Law, Light, and Liberty

J. H. COURT, Ph.D.

Senior Lecturer in Psychology,
Flinders University, South Australia

Chi Rho

Lutheran Publishing House, Adelaide

Printed and Published by
Lutheran Publishing House,
205 Halifax Street, Adelaide, Aust.

First Published June 1975

ISBN 0 85910 026 X

Preface

The rapid changes occurring in community standards may be seen around the world. The core of this book originally appeared as a commentary on such changes occurring in Australia under the title, "Changing Community Standards". It was provoked by a state of confusion arising from a changed policy on censorship at the national level, together with a diversity of policies operating within the States of Australia.

Such local issues have their counterparts in other countries, and the more fundamental questions relating to personal freedom and social responsibility deserve wide consideration. The original material has therefore been extended to take account of these wider issues and to relate the findings of science to the values of Christian morality. In this way it is hoped that positive recommendations will emerge whereby the individual citizen can make an informed contribution to an area of debate, the outcome of which will significantly influence the kind of world our children will live in. In the three-year interval since "Changing Community Standards" appeared, there has been an impressive development of public response to moral issues, such that they are the subject of more serious and informed debate than has been customary.

It should be noted that, in proposing several principles that might be upheld, the approach is very different from much of what is commonly done when difficult political decisions arise. All too often we find action taken to handle a crisis which simply seeks an immediate solution, while general principles are disregarded. Such tactics buy short-term results at the expense of long-term confusion. Just as a doctor must treat not only the present symptom but also the underlying condition, so, too, an approach to issues like censorship must ask, "What principles shall be applied?" Much censorship has been held up to ridicule due to *ad hoc* decisions. It may not be easy to work from generally-agreed principles to particular applications, but it is this deductive approach which will prove most acceptable in the long run.

This book goes far beyond the issue of censorship. It seeks to examine, in addition, numerous influences which may have adverse effects on society because they pose a threat to morality. Although examples are largely derived from Australia, a wider application is intended. In preparing this book, the author has visited and consulted with experts in New Zealand, the United States, Britain, and Scandinavia. Challenges to the law, and the contentious issue of liberty, are of international importance. Decisions made in one country rapidly influence decisions in other parts of the world. This fact is both a challenge and an encouragement for those who care enough about liberty to exercise their democratic rights responsibly.

April 1975. John H. Court.

DEDICATED TO CHILDREN,

whose happiness and hopes for tomorrow

are being shaped today.

Contents

1

A Time of Change

Water-pollution and air-pollution are now quantitatively measurable facts of life, but it also appears that an insidious psychological poison is permeating the modern consciousness, destroying man's mind and moral fibre.

D. Williams in 'Trousered Apes'

To say that community-acceptance has changed in recent years is to say nothing new. In every area, from standards of dress to standards of living, from quality of literature to quality of water, we know that things have dramatically altered, not merely in our lifetime, but even over a five-year period. Change may be good, bad, or neutral; but one would hope that the general trend for society would be for the better. Recently Sir Elwyn Jones, the former British Attorney-General, speaking of growing consciousness of environmental pollution problems, said, "It is paradoxical that, at such a time, there should also be a movement for the abandonment of any control of the cultural pollution represented by obscenity". In the world of ecology there does seem to be a sufficient consensus of gloom for the Australian Post Office to frank our letters with the caption "Pollution: Cause for Common Concern". The idea of pollution well conveys what is happening also in moral and psychological areas. We are in danger of reacting too slowly there also, just as we are only now becoming conscious of the life-threatening changes that have occurred, almost unnoticed, in our physical world.

It is the slow, creeping change which is hardest to detect and hardest to fight. The causes are difficult to isolate, and harm is well advanced before effective action is taken. By the time the effects of change are great enough to be clear, it often appears too late to do anything. That has been the story with polluted rivers and smoke-laden air. It is true, too, of polluted minds.

TIME TO TAKE STOCK

Before we are overwhelmed by these slow but relentless changes, we must take stock. Standards of community-acceptance have changed beyond recognition in recent years. At first slowly, but now with increasing momentum, we are accepting as normal what would once have been unthinkable. "A good thing", someone says, "we're growing more mature". Yet so much of the evidence indicates quite the reverse. Indeed, so dramatic are some of the statistics of personal distress and social disorganization that we may say that many of the changes represent not the vigorous growth of a healthy life, but rather the galloping symptoms of a fast-decaying organism.

The actual statistics of change vary from place to place, but the trends show a depressing similarity. A few examples from here and there may serve as a reminder that even small changes, when they continue, become highly significant.

In the United States, the probability that a girl would be the victim of rape doubled over a ten-year period. Violence has erupted so obviously that it is reportedly more dangerous to walk in some cities there than in war-ravaged Saigon. In Australia, reported rape rose by 39% in one year, while over a ten-year period in South Australia it has risen by 400%.

From London it is reported that half-a-million children are known to be battered or neglected in Britain each year. In the United States, baby-battering reportedly runs at 80,000 per year, while homicide exceeds 16,000 per year.

From Sydney has come a report that gambling in New South Wales involved an annual turnover of $3,240 million. Such a figure must be condemned as immoral, for a population of under five million.

IMITATORS OF VIOLENCE

Violence is also the subject of gradual attitude-change as it permeates theatre and television screens more and more. The Report on television prepared by the Surgeon-General in America found that the average 16-year-old could be expected to have seen 18,000 people killed on the screen. A BBC report from Britain gave an analysis of 1,558 programs, and found them to contain 1,889 incidents of violence, giving an average of one every half-hour. That intensity appears to be even greater in Australia. As it is now well-established that young people will commonly imitate the violence they see (especially if there is no punishment following the violent act, and the viewer has tensions seeking release), it comes as no surprise that violent crime in Australia among young people trebled over a 12-year period. Of this rise, a police superintendent said, "The aggressive spate of increased crime is particularly prevalent in the 15- to 19-years age-group. We are entering an era of change and deteriorating moral standards." Of the same trend, a professor of education said, "It is possible films, drama, and art works that put forward an abnormal viewpoint contribute. I believe lack of discipline and guidance are contributing causes to the rising crime rate."

It has been proposed by the sociologist Sorokin in his book, "The American Sex Revolution", that disorganized standards of sexual morality are associated with an increase of mental illness. He developed his view from a study of Russia, and the argument is by no means clear-cut because of problems of detection and reporting-rates. Nevertheless, it is serious when the fastest growth in psychiatric populations in America proves to be among the 10-14 age-group, where total numbers have doubled in less than ten years.

Abortions in the State of New York run in excess of 200,000 per year, and are carried out even as late as 26 weeks after conception; something like one-third of these are performed on teenagers.

More than 19,000 illegitimate babies are born to Australian mothers each year. And there are over 1,000 new cases of venereal disease each week, of whom about one-third are teenagers.

Who can say where the causes lie? They are multiple, of course; but there can be no doubt that this accumulation is to the detriment of society.

To this sad catalogue, one can only too easily add the mushrooming drug problem, vandalism, shoplifting, and other indications that a sense of personal responsibility is sadly lacking. It would be naive to suppose that there are simple explanations or simple solutions to such massive signs of social upheaval. Yet some attempts **must** be made to detect basic reasons for such a consistent trend.

The blithe belief that education, the reduction of poverty, or the provision of adequate social welfare facilities would solve society's problems, has patently been disproved. Many constructive and beneficial reforms have occurred in Western countries; economically there has been great progress; yet, with remarkable consistency, while material standards have advanced, moral standards have declined.

It would be impossible to explore all these areas of change, and to analyse their significance in detail. The outcome, even if expertly achieved, would be so extensive as to be overwhelming. Attention will therefore be directed to more restricted areas which can be carefully documented to pinpoint some of the changes in community standards that have occurred. Reasons why they have occurred will be offered, and every effort will be made to distinguish between fact and opinion.

THE COMMUNITY STANDARDS WATERSHED

The term "community standards" became of public importance in June 1970. About six months after Mr. Don Chipp became the Liberal Minister for Customs and Excise, he delivered a policy speech in the House of Representatives in Canberra, which was apparently the first statement on the topic of censorship in the House since 1938. It is doubtful whether more than a handful of the community realized how radical that statement was, or how far-reaching the consequences. In that speech, the Minister made clear his intention to base censorship decisions on his evaluation of currently-prevailing community standards.

Prior to that speech, material was commonly excluded from Australia if it dealt with sexual behaviour or violence in an unacceptable way. In earlier years the criterion was whether or not scenes depicting such matters "were likely to encourage depravity". However, the laws of Australia and other countries have had the greatest difficulty in proving that any material will encourage depravity. As recently as 1968, Judge Windeyer stated, "It is assumed incontravertibly by the common law that obscene writings do degrade and corrupt morals . . .", but since then there has been even less willingness to make such assumptions, or for that matter to say what is meant by obscene.

Faced, then, with such difficulties, some alternative criteria for censorship were sought. The Minister in 1970 came out in support for the concept of contemporary community standards, backed by such research as might assist him and his advisers. The appeal to community standards was not actually new; in effect, this had been used for some time, following a U.S. court case of 1957; but the explicit acceptance of this principle makes it necessary to determine its merits.

In the wake of the new criteria, obvious changes in the standards of material publicly available could be detected. The foundations were laid for a steady erosion of standards to the point where eventually the concept of censorship might be quietly abolished.

AN ACCELERATED DECLINE

The decline was accelerated when the Liberal Government went out of office in December 1972, to be replaced by the Labor Government. The Federal control of books and films moved into the hands of the-then Senator Lionel Murphy. He proceeded to implement as rapidly as possible a new basis for decisions as contained in the Labor Party platform. Instead of seeking some assessment of community standards, the new terminology stated:

> "Adults should be entitled to read, hear and view what they wish in private or public, and that persons and those in their care be protected from exposure to unsolicited material offensive to them."

This definition has the appearance of ignoring all idea of standards, and yet it has been applied with an acknowledgement that the portrayal of violence could be socially dangerous and must be subject to some restraint. Consequently, the potential sex-offender can pursue his literary delights unimpeded, on the grounds that his personal freedom to choose must be maintained, while the potential assassin has his freedom restrained. There might be some logic in this if it could be shown that the likelihood of imitation was high with one type of behaviour but not with the other. In actual fact, in spite of many trite assertions by humanists, the evidence more strongly favours the view that restraint is justified in both areas.[1]

The situation therefore has developed that one man's private view of what we should or should not see replaces the system of safeguards and controls which previously operated. More recently Senator

Murphy has been elected to the High Court of Australia, and thus no longer bears responsibility for government policy or decisions in this area. He has been succeeded by Mr. K. Enderby, who is expected to hew the same path. If he adopts Senator Murphy's previously-stated stance that hard-core pornography become available to those who wish to obtain it, the question of criteria and standards remains an important one.

It is for those who believe that good standards have existed and should be maintained to take a firm stand against those who proclaim that there are no dangers in abandoning those standards. What people see and read influences the way they think and act. There are ample indications that public behaviour is a matter for concern, and many wonder if any remedies are to hand. One could wish to see an application of the words of the Prime Minister, Mr. Whitlam, in his Australia Day speech for 1974:

> "Let us resolve that we will never tolerate a nation of second-hand standards or second-hand ideas. . . . Let us commit ourselves to a greater Australia . . . generously out of regard for the welfare of our fellow-man and our neighbours. We will not be judged by the songs we sing but by our behaviour as a people."

2

Contemporary Community Standards

Revolutionary changes have taken place in attitudes towards what may properly be discussed in newspapers, on radio, and on television. . . . But some standards remain, and we are charged with the duty of saying what they are.

Mr. Justice Wells

As we reflect on so many different kinds of disturbed behaviour in society, the question arises, "Can anything be done?". Hopefully, there is one major point at which influence can be brought to bear: the exercising of control over what moulds the minds of those who are susceptible to corruption.

The news media have become the powerful vehicle by which community attitudes and opinions are shaped. As they progressively come to be owned by a small group of people, so the risk of calculated distortion increases. If democracy thrives on a free exchange of true information, we should be concerned that it is possible for large sections of the community to be deceived.

Together with the news media, the entertainment world must be increasingly identified as a powerful force shaping contemporary opinion. Films and plays do not merely reflect the current scene, but actually mould it. Both individual people and society as a whole will move toward the portrayal of fiction as the dividing-line between fantasy and reality becomes more blurred. As films and books become more graphic, we must be seriously concerned at their preoccupation with what is sick, morbid, and obsessive, rather than with the promotion of values the society endorses. In the name of "reality" we have all that is sick presented in magnified detail.

A CASE FOR QUALITY CONTROL

It is against the hazards that arise from such morbid preoccupation, that censorship can most readily be seen to be justified. Because of its potential for abuse, censorship has become a loaded word, and many reject it without further thought. We therefore prefer to advocate "quality control", in order to express the need to preserve high standards by the exclusion of whatever does not measure up.

Unfortunately, the burning question which arises is, "What shall be the standard?". Here lies much of the contemporary problem. Judgements and standards established in the law courts, and based on assumptions of Christian morality, have been challenged — and in some places rejected. Departing from this set of values, society has no agreed alternatives. The ultimate logical conclusion is to say that no decisions can be made, and anything goes! In the confused situation, however, the law is making a compromise effort to find some basis for decisions, as it is recognized that there is much to offend, disgust, or harm being widely peddled in the name of freedom.

Progressively we have moved to the point where the decisions on what shall be allowed are taken in terms of what the community is believed to want. This is, of course, an arbitrary and shifting standard, sufficiently vague to be ideally suited to those who wish to test the limits of the law. Both the pornographer who is out to make money, and the malcontent eager to challenge law and order, can make capital out of the uncertainties of such ill-defined standards.

MILESTONES ALONG THE WAY

A few milestones are worth mentioning to show the efforts that have been made to draw a line between the acceptable and the unacceptable. They relate, in the main, to the areas of obscenity and pornography.

In England, the provisions of the Obscene Publications Act of 1857 were updated in 1959. A working statement, formulated by Chief Justice Cockburn in 1868 to enable magistrates to determine what is obscene, continued to be applied:

> "I think the test of obscenity is this, whether the tendency of the matter charged as obscenity is to deprave and corrupt those whose minds are open to such immoral influences, and into whose hands a publication of this sort might fall."[1]

In the United States, a major legal event was the case of Roth v U.S. in 1956-7, in which a book-dealer was charged with using the mail to traffic in obscenity. Tests of material in terms of "social value" and "prurient interest" were spelled out. The social value assessment stated:

> "All ideas having even the slightest redeeming social importance —unorthodox ideas, controversial ideas, even ideas hateful to the prevailing climate of opinion — have the full protection of the guarantees, unless excludable because they encroach upon the limited area of more important interests. But implicit in the history of the First Amendment is the rejection of obscenity as utterly without redeeming social importance."[2]

The assessment of prurient interest stated:

> "Obscene material is material which deals with sex in a manner appealing to prurient interest. . . . A thing is obscene if,

considered as a whole, its predominant appeal is to prurient interest, i.e. a shameful or morbid interest in nudity, sex, or excretion, and if it goes substantially beyond customary limits of such matters."[3]

It was from the continuation of the Roth case that there developed the appeal to community standards. Klausler describes this as follows:

"[Roth] was tried in New York and found guilty. Thereupon he appealed to the U.S. Supreme Court, which upheld his conviction. In its opinion the Court declared that in determining what is obscene it must be determined 'whether to the average person, applying contemporary community standards, the dominant theme of the material taken as a whole appeals to prurient interest'. A few years later the Court added a further test when it declared obscene material must not only appeal to 'prurient interest' but must also be patently offensive to community standards of decency. . . . Obviously this additional criterion adds to the confusion, for who is to determine what the 'community standards of decency' are?"

Who indeed? Yet it has not deterred others from imitating.

In Australia, the Federal law traditionally tried to establish what was "likely to encourage depravity". It has of course been difficult to prove that material causes depravity. As recently as 1968, Judge Windeyer stated in the Australian High Court (in the case of Crowe v Graham and others):

"It is assumed incontravertibly by the common law that obscene writings do degrade and corrupt morals. . . ." [4]

The major event since then on the Australian scene has been the adoption of the American principle of using community standards to determine the acceptability of published material.

CAN THE CRITERION STAND?

The implications of this decision are worth following through, so that the limitations of this approach can be clearly seen.

The acceptance of this criterion poses several formidable — perhaps insuperable — problems, some of which were mentioned in the Minister's speech in Parliament in June 1970. For example:

"Community standards are most difficult to define. In fact, one may ask whether 'community standards' exist at all. Are they representative of the standards of the entire adult population or are they a broad assessment of what people believe to be right? . . . I believe that community standards can be understood and defined only if there is continuing public discussion of censorship, and only if a broad and representative section of the adult population makes its views known."

The sentiments sound fine and splendidly democratic. But we need to enquire whether they are realistic or idealistic.

There are several reasons why the criterion of "prevailing community standards" cannot work effectively at this time in our society.

1. The first question posed by the Minister in regard to community standards was, "Are they representative of the standards of the entire adult population?" There **is** no single community standard against which to assess anything. We live in a heterogeneous, pluralist society with many opinions, attitudes, and philosophies. It is conceivable that one might find an identifiable community-standard in a totalitarian society, but the concept is meaningless in a contemporary Western-style democracy.

2. The alternative question of the Minister was, "Are they a broad assessment of what most people believe to be right?" Here the criterion becomes one of morality — in effect, one of Christian morality, since the large majority of the population identifies itself with the Christian faith. If clear statements of Christian morality could be prepared that would provide practical guides to what is right, this might indeed serve as a valuable framework for Ministerial decisions. There is little doubt that the informed Christian does have views which, if fully formulated, could provide a basis for decision-making. But the beliefs of most people cannot be said to be explicitly Christian in spite of a nominal adherence to the Christian faith. Hans Mol[5] finds that less than half of the population are regular church-goers; no doubt the percentage able to offer a clear defence of Christian standards of morality would be substantially less. So it does not appear that one can hope to get a proper assessment from the community as to what it believes to be **right**.

THE TRAP OF COMMUNITY OPINION

3. Failing these sources, the alternative proposed is to get as wide a cross-section of opinion as possible. Here the assumption is that by pooling all the available opinions, a common denominator will emerge, and the detection of this will yield the most satisfactory criterion. Such a belief is as naive as it is dangerous, for several reasons.

(a) Such a means of assessment, even if truly representative, could only yield the **lowest** common denominator. Decisions would have to be based on a massive compromise in order to accommodate all shades of opinion.

(b) The method assumes that people are active and interested enough to respond constantly on every issue that comes to their attention. Since Mr. Chipp himself said that people in Australia rated censorship as eleventh in a list of priorities, it is clear that people generally would not provide the kind of reaction he sought.

(c) This leaves open the high probability that such feedback as is received will not be truly representative, but based on vested interests. It is very much to the advantage of book publishers and film producers to give vocal support to more liberal censorship. It is even worth their while to spend thousands of dollars to get this message to the Minister and his advisers.

But the large majority of the community has neither time nor resources to express whatever view it may have. So it is a matter for frequent debate as to *who the majority is*. Is it a majority who seek more permissiveness, or is this a minority wish? In a sober and balanced review of current trends, Gummer states that "the demand for most of the permissive changes in legislation has been a limited one, confined to an articulate group and rarely gaining the support of the 'silent majority'. It is difficult to discern any widespread desire in any Western country for the abolition of the laws governing pornography, yet in most countries there is an active and well-organized pressure-group to do just this. Most changes in moral legislation have been put through without forming any significant part of the ruling party's election manifesto. . . . Usually there is no opportunity for the public to choose. In Denmark the Conservative coalition government which removed all censorship on pornographic literature, not only did so without any mandate from the electorate, but it announced its decision without any vote in Parliament."[6] In Britain, significant changes in moral areas have been introduced through private members' bills rather than through the usual party-initiated channels. The same tactic has been adopted in Australia in order to change the laws on homosexuality.

(d) Furthermore, the average man and woman cannot make the kind of informed judgements that the criterion of community standards demands. If it has proved so difficult for expert advisers to decide whether material may be harmful to the community, why should we expect the average man to do better? He does not necessarily know what he wants; he recognizes he has not been trained to know, and he certainly cannot be relied upon to choose what will be best for him and the community. We are accustomed to relying on expert opinion in areas of public health, and do not ask for community decisions on matters like pharmaceuticals or vaccination. The criteria for censorship, being the more difficult, should with more justice be handled by experts.

(e) Even supposing the community was willing and able to express a prevailing community standard, the means of doing so would still be totally unworkable. The decision whether a film or a book or a play is acceptable must be made on the basis of evidence. For the community to judge, all must therefore be exposed to it so that all can respond. That requirement conflicts with the requirement to restrain whatever might prove harmful. We cannot judge without seeing, but by then it is too late to do anything. So if this principle is followed logically, the Customs Department should be releasing everything without restriction, yet be willing to withdraw material on the basis of a majority dissent. We see great pressure for implementing the first part of this approach, but no evidence of machinery to handle withdrawal of material when this is necessary.

(f) Implicit also in the "community standards" criterion is the assumption that if the majority wants something, that is justification for making it available. That the majority is always right is a dubious principle even if applied scrupulously; but where a minority group stands to make money out of making its viewpoint appear to be the desire of the majority, the assumption cannot be relied on.

(g) The mechanics of the operation make the whole system unworkable. Mr. Chipp said it could work "only if a broad and representative section of the adult population makes its views known". This is true; but is it realistic to expect **millions** to keep writing in with their opinion? One says "millions", because anything less can so readily be disregarded as a minority viewpoint.

THE LIGHT OF EXPERIENCE

4. Evidence from applying the "community standards" criterion elsewhere is also not encouraging. In the United States, the indications are that the standards shift, and the direction is down. In regard to this, Grim refers to the experience of "The San Francisco Examiner":

> "The Supreme Court decreed, for example, that 'community standards' should determine what is and what is not obscene. But, declared the editors: 'After witnessing the results of the decision, we are now convinced that community standards do not determine what is pornography. Quite the contrary. We believe the results in San Francisco are proof positive that proliferating pornography creates depravity that can — and does — breed moral pollution and social degeneracy.' " [7]

So great do the above limitations appear that one must question whether that 1970 policy speech has been either misrepresented or misunderstood. A few sentences from a statement of November 1971 should clarify the matter.

This statement was made in reply to representations of the national body in Australia called Community Standards Organization, which was seeking to present a community viewpoint to the Minister.

> "The point was made strongly in the Minister's statement in June 1970, that in censorship 'the criteria emphasis has been shifted from the tendency to deprave and corrupt to the community standards, which is the tacit involvement of the community'. In other words, a book or film is regarded as obscene if its content is offensive to contemporary community standards of decency. . . . Simply stated, censorship in 1970 is a matter of community taste."

In 1975, the situation is quite different again. The extended application of a totally-unworkable system has so eroded prevailing standards, that the new Government was able to make sweeping changes without effective challenge.

WHERE WE STAND NOW

Whereas in 1970 explicitness was defended, but any suggestion of permitting pornography to circulate was rejected, 1975 offers even less restraints. The hypocrisy of the whole sequence has progressively unfolded. First it was "no pornography"; then it was "no hard-core pornography"; then it was "some hard-core pornography, but with restrictions on violence". All the time, despite the public statements, the reality was a step ahead, preparing the way for a further erosion.

By January 1974, Senator Murphy was ready to call Ministers of the States together to accept hard-core pornography with only token limitations. It was proposed that "publications which are considered to be 'hard-core' pornography will be classified for direct sale only. These publications cannot be sold to anyone except by mail, and in single copies to adults."[8]

Several State Ministers had initially made strong statements rejecting such an idea; but, on going to Canberra, all but Mr. Knox of Queensland accepted the classification proposals on an advisory basis.

A further category of restriction makes clear where we are really placed in 1975. Officially "publications which advocate or incite to crime, violence, or the use of illegal drugs will be prohibited". In reality, this means that such material is already circulating relatively freely, and will shortly be given the official blessing that the present Government now bestows on hard-core pornography.

Public statements that there is no longer any censorship in Australia now go unchallenged. This is true in the strict sense of pre-publication censorship. It is also tragically true that material which is degrading, offensive, and inciting to civil disorder, also circulates without restraint. As such material is allowed to permeate society, so the values of the community continue to be undermined. Community taste is changing its meaning from something worthy to something debased.

It is clear that the wide availability of printed material which has developed during the past century poses conflicts of interests in society to which solutions are not easily found. The appeal to community standards has not proved itself to be effective in balancing the needs of all groups in an acceptable fashion. Other approaches deserve attention. A comparison of the laws in the United States, Britain, Australia, and New Zealand has been published by Dearn.[9] His is the critique of a practising lawyer who believes there is a need for control over published material. He writes favourably of the New Zealand system involving an Indecent Publications Tribunal. He concludes that "the New Zealand Tribunal has much to commend itself. It is superior to the majority of Boards or Committees inasmuch as it has clear statutory guidelines of an autonomous nature. It also provides necessary safeguards to enable appeals to be made to Courts of law."

3

Community Taste

In those days . . . every man did what was right in his own eyes. *Judges 21.25*

If community standards — or, even more arbitrarily, community taste — is the criterion, who judges this nebulous quality? The seemingly-democratic basis for decision actually resolves itself as the conclusions of the Minister and his advisers in the Department of Customs and Excise. Since the activities of the National Literature Board of Review and the Film Censorship Board are made public, we know something of the decisions that are made, but this is as far as the democratic process goes. The opinions of the man-in-the-street will not change policy at that level since the boards are made up of experts paid to do the job. Very properly, their opinions are given greater weight than are those of other interested but less well-informed parties.

A central body cannot hope always to be exactly in line with something that is so ill-defined and so ephemeral. Hence Mr. Chipp said he would sometimes be a little behind, sometimes a little ahead of, public opinion, relying on feedback from the community to know where he stood. Since his general view of censorship was that it is evil and undesirable, it would surely follow that changes in standards would be in the direction of less censorship rather than more, and with the goal of its ultimate removal. By setting up a system which prevents any adequate assessment of whether decisions are generally approved, the decisions of a department can always be made to appear as if they were wise. If challenged, rather than to admit a mistake, it is more strategic to threaten resignation.

THE REAL BASES FOR DECISIONS

In reality, therefore, what is publicly proclaimed as a policy of responding to contemporary community standards, in fact draws on two rather different criteria. One is the personal philosophy of the Minister; the other is a reliance on such scientific or legal evidence as may be available to his advisers. The personal philosophy is placed first since this appears to be given more weight. Even granting that standards do change, the-then Minister acknowledged that these changes are not keeping pace with the changes in what mass media are seeking to present. In his June 1970 speech he said, "However, community standards are broadening at a slower rate than the rate of permissiveness (in films and publications), not only in content but in themes attempted. The gap between the two grows wider." Should not the admission of a widening gap be an argument for moving more slowly? Instead, the period since that speech has been marked by an accelerated pace rather than by restraint.

The lists of released books, issued at regular intervals, indicate availability of much that was previously prohibited. Most of these changes have been justified in terms of the freedom of choice of mature adults. The release of "The Little Red School Book" broke new ground by freeing material explicitly aimed at the young. Regardless of any opinion one may hold of that book, it is instructive to read how the Minister proposed to respond to the community's representations. According to an extended interview reported in the Melbourne "Herald" of March 16, 1972:

> "He has sweated over his decision. . . . He does not find the book subversive. . . . He waits for the usual moral terriers to snap at his heels. . . . This intelligent, aggressive, but smooth Minister will not dismiss things out of hand, just because they are not liked."

If this was a true reflection of the position, it appears that the criterion of community taste was abandoned in favour of a personal decision. The decision provoked a crisis in the Cabinet in which Mr. Chipp's decision was narrowly upheld. As a reversal would undoubtedly have caused the Government to fall, some have cynically concluded that the welfare of children is prized less than the survival of the Government.

THE 'R' CERTIFICATE FIASCO

The Chipp era also saw the introduction of 'R' certificate films. With the justification that some serious themes deserve treatment in a manner appropriate only for adult audiences, this category of films brought to Australia a whole flood of material that had previously been excluded or heavily cut. There are apparently high-minded civil libertarians who believe we are now more mature for the experience.

In actual fact, this certificate for the most part has provided one more excuse for lowering the community standards of taste and morality. Far from presenting serious themes in a mature fashion, the 'R' certificate has become identifiable with all that is bawdy, perverse, and violent. The films in this category pander to lust, and incite all-too-many viewers to act out their sick fantasies on others.

The hypocrisy surrounding the system may be seen in various ways. Those who proclaim civil liberties and the rights of citizens to be free from offence are, in this area, the ones most guilty of thrusting into the community that which many abhor. Films like "The Devils", "Last Tango in Paris", and "A Clockwork Orange" have been introduced in spite of strenuous objections from many quarters. Even community taste has been overridden in order to please those selfish individuals who irresponsibly demand their own way, wanting to feed their minds with corrupt ideas.

The 'R' certificate supposedly provides a protection for young people who, it was recognized, could be emotionally harmed by such films. Here, too, the hypocrisy has become only too apparent. An age-restriction between the ages of six and 18 was initially applied in most States. The lower age of six was a grotesquely bad choice, since the four- and five-year-olds would be among the ones most likely to suffer harm. Shocked by unfamiliar experiences and lacking the vocabulary to express their feelings, they suffer long-term effects which may never be fully known. It took two years to revise the law and to reduce the lower limit to two years of age.

At the other end, even more of a fiasco has occurred. Even though State and Federal ministers have repeatedly been advised that the age-limits are not being applied, little legal action has been undertaken. To the end of 1973, only one conviction had occurred in the whole of Australia.

THE DRIVE-IN THEATRE LOOPHOLE

Even if the age-restrictions were carefully enforced, this is still no answer to the drive-in theatre. Those who live near such theatres know how many young people sit around the perimeter to view the screen. The visual impact of contemporary films provides sufficient stimulus to encourage this practice unless it is specifically prevented. To acknowledge that such films can harm, and yet to allow such open access to them, is indefensible. Those who truly want freedom for the adult, while recognizing a responsibility to the young, need to exert pressure for control over all these loopholes. Nominated indoor theatres could provide adult freedom without all these undesirable and unnecessary complications. If only certain specified theatres showed 'R' films, the pressure to compete commercially would also be reduced; and the average citizen could, in addition, be spared the aggressive advertising which currently defaces many daily papers.

In 1974 we moved explicitly beyond the criterion of community taste in this area. A notable landmark occurred in December 1973, when the film, "Language of Love", was released on the personal decision of Senator Murphy. The choice was a careful one, and so timed to make a public reaction difficult. The film was viewed by a few members of Parliament on the evening that the House rose for the Christmas recess. It was not a film that could be criticized for its violence or any dramatically anti-social components. It was a documentary "sex-education" film with a humanistic philosophy.

The significance of the decision lies not in its content, but in the way in which previous criteria of release were discarded. In Mr. Chipp's time as Minister, the film had been rejected as pornographic. The Commonwealth Film Censorship Board declared it should not receive an 'R' certificate. On appeal, the Film Board of Review upheld that decision. However, Senator Murphy chose to exercise his ministerial prerogative and personally decided the film should be released.

AN OMINOUS DANGER

Such a precedent is ominous for the future. If such autocratic decisions go unchallenged, democracy is threatened. If Senator Murphy's indication that he is keen to see pornographic films made available to those who want them is taken up by his successor, it takes little imagination to anticipate the future trend in films.

The sad thing about this determination to allow even the most obscene material to circulate, is that it is masquerading in the name of freedom. It is being done, moreover, at a time when those in Britain and America who have blazed this very trail are withdrawing. While we are lowering restraints and abandoning standards, those countries are having second thoughts on the wisdom of such a course. Faced with mounting evidence of serious harm from such a policy, they are now undertaking a tightening of laws on pornography. Without wishing to put the clock back, it would be good for Australia at least to avoid breaking the mainspring.

4

A Pattern of Change

The world has changed in the last decades . . . increasingly we see ourselves living in a world that is post-Christian and even post-humanist, a neo-pagan world, one which is nihilist, or anarchist, or mystic. H.R. Rookmaaker

Changes in standards of content and presentation in the mass media are not accidental. Nor do they flow from spur-of-the-moment ideas which can be lightly dismissed as short-lived or insignificant. The propagating of similar themes in films, books, plays, radio, and TV indicates that an underlying philosophy of life, or an ideology, is finding expression. It extends beyond national boundaries and is sufficiently prevalent to suggest that it represents an attitude which, if not widely endorsed, at least has the benefit of powerful promotion.

Until the end of World War II, and perhaps in certain places for some time after that, the set of values most widely subscribed to in the Western world was essentially Christian. The guiding principles adopted by mass media, and the expression of public opinion found in the law and politics, were clearly derived from Christian teaching. The dignity of life, special care for women, responsibility for the needs of children and the disadvantaged, are examples of the values that were self-evidently accepted.

Due to many factors which extend well beyond the scope of this book, the last twenty-five years have seen a departure from such assumptions that is more radical than many realize. A few of the contributing factors are worth mentioning to illustrate why there are sharp differences in viewpoint among different groups in the community.

FACTORS INFLUENCING CHANGE

Some have distinguished the younger generation as having a different life-view from their parents. This "generation gap" does appear to have a greater significance than the differences in outlook which have always been evident between parents and children.

It is an interesting proposition that there was a watershed associated with the exploding of the first atomic bomb. This demonstration of mass destruction so shifted the view of how war might be conducted, that the generation growing up since that momentous event has inevitably contemplated life and death from beneath the psychological fallout of the bomb. Reactions against the inhumanity of mass-warfare have served as a catalyst to bring both the frustrated and the idealistic together in marches and demonstrations associated with the peace symbol.

However, it is impossible to distinguish clearly between the forces generated by that reorientation of outlook, and the very significant shift which took place concurrently in child-rearing practices.

The present young adult population started life in the years from 1940 onwards, and hence spent formative years in the post-war period. That in itself could explain why an attitude of rejection of authority of parents and governments might spring up. But, more particularly, the period of the 50s and 60s saw the heyday of free expression as an approach to child-rearing practices. The theories of Freud were widely accepted, especially in intellectual families, and the concept of repression was considered to be particularly dangerous to healthy emotional development. The belief that repression is fundamentally bad, is now the prevailing influence in today's young-adult generation which rejects controls even more vigorously. Unfortunately, the repression theory has been misapplied and is counter-productive. [1]

Concurrent with changes in the home, there have been major changes also in educational philosophy and practice. In reaction against the more restrictive practices which could inhibit emotional, social, and cognitive growth, there has been increasing encouragement given to freedom of expression and development of independence. There have been undoubted benefits from this rethinking and effort to create a more stimulating environment for children. But, as so often happens, what started as a healthy corrective has widely developed into a cult as extreme as the practice which triggered it. The climate of opinion which was ready for change of a healthy kind also allowed the emergence of extreme trends. And these are now creating real difficulties as the products of this emphasis find their way into the adult world.

EXTREME TRENDS IN EDUCATION

Perhaps the best-known and extreme version of this trend has been that explored by A.S. Neill at Summerhill. From a special situation, pioneered by a special sort of person, efforts have been made to generalize and to argue that a pattern which solved some problems can provide wider solutions in many other contexts.

To understand the total impact of this philosophy, it is important to identify the background to this approach. An evaluation of Neill's recommendations regarding freedom in the school situation should be made in terms of his overall philosophy. Radical changes in the way children are educated are not advocated in a vacuum, but clearly have some goals in mind. A brief summary of Neill's philosophy is as follows:

1. Adults have no right to insist on obedience from their children.
2. Children must not be asked to work at all until they reach eighteen years of age.
3. Religion should not be taught to children.
4. Punishment of any kind is strictly forbidden. A parent who spanks his child actually hates him, and his desire to hurt the child results from his own unsatisfied sex life.
5. Adolescents should be told sexual promiscuity is not a moral issue at all.
6. No pornographic books or materials should be withheld from the child.
7. Children should not be required to say "thank you" or "please" to their parents.
8. Rewarding a child for good behaviour is a degrading and demoralizing practice.

These points are a summary of a fuller description given by Dobson, an American psychologist, who then comments:

> "He represents an entire era, dominated by the neo-Freudians who reigned during the 1950s and early 1960s. The painful impact of those years will not soon fade. Most of the values held tightly by the 'now' generation were implanted during the period I have described. Please note how many of the following elements of the new morality can be traced to the permissive viewpoint represented by Neill: God is dead; immorality is wonderful; nudity is noble; irresponsibility is groovy; disrespect and irreverence are fashionable; unpopular laws are to be disobeyed; violence is an acceptable vehicle for bringing change; authority is evil; everyone over thirty is stupid; pleasure is paramount; diligence is distasteful . . ."[2]

THE ARENA OF THE COMING GENERATION

In identifying the push towards children's rights, one should note that several philosophies converge. The movement is strongly supported by humanism in its most recent manifesto.[3] The political motivation for it has been extensively documented as springing from Trotskyist and Maoist organizations. Agitation among school students, and , most obviously, the message of "The Little Red School Book", arises from the determination of the political extreme-left to take over the coming generation.

Swerling writes of the Children's Rights Campaign in Britain:

> "This propaganda campaign was the brainchild of the National Council for Civil Liberties. It gathered momentum in 1970 with an initiative aimed at giving children some say in decisions affecting their schooling. . . The Children's Committee of the NCCL have advocated that children should be free to have sexual intercourse whenever they wish . . . the trend towards sexual permissiveness is consistent with the growth of civil liberties."

Those who think the move towards children's rights is a wise and democratic one would do well to see that the title is no more than a deceptive mask for subversion. The British movement now has a magazine entitled "Children's Rights", which in its first issue addressed its young readers, saying:

> "Education can damage your mind . . . we are tired of being a repressed generation. Our generation is repressed by censorship laws, age regulations, school, and sadly our own parents. No longer shall we accept this repression. We are angry. The only hope for a future society lies in us. The present system of indoctrination will fail to make way for the new real education. The reprinting of an uncensored 'Little Red Schoolbook' for free distribution was our first act. We shall not limit ourselves to non-violent acts if the school situation persists. . . . All sabotage is effective in hierarchical systems like schools — smash tannoys [P.A. systems], paint blackboards red, grind all the chalk to dust: you're angry — you know what to do."

A predictable development of this philosophy is the emergence of a clamour for children's rights. Each step appears to follow logically and rationally from what has gone before. It is only by tracing the trends back to their beginnings that one can identify the inherent dangers. The clamour for children's rights is as unbalanced as have been past efforts to make children the slaves of their elders. As Mary Whitehouse said:

> "Public opinion long ago condemned and outlawed the exploitation of child-labour by nineteenth-century industrialists. Yet today, our society ruthlessly exploits the minds and emotions of young people for financial and political capital. Children are fodder not for industry, but for ideas. They are no longer sent up chimneys, but they're pressurized into alien patterns of behaviour to line the pockets of unscrupulous publishers and to further the cause of revolution by stealth."[4]

The children's rights movement appears to disregard both the need for responsibility, and the fact that both rights and responsibility can be exercised maturely only in the context of appropriate experience and training. Of course, if the older generation has nothing of value to impart to its children, it follows that no clear guidance and training can be offered. But such a bankrupt attitude to adult responsibility must surely be an indictment indeed. Interwoven with these forces has been the upsurge of important ideological changes. That there has been a widespread departure from Christian belief is self-evident. The reasons for this are legion; many explanations might be offered, each correct to a point, but none sufficient in itself.

Disillusionment following war might be a partial explanation in Britain with its post-war struggles to regain stability; but this would be difficult to demonstrate in other countries, like America or Australia, where the impact of war was very different. And yet the trend is rather similar.

Another major force at work has been the explosion of knowledge and increased educational opportunity. With half of the world's scientific knowledge said to have been derived over the last fifteen years, there must clearly be some readjustments in people's evaluation of the importance of scientific truth. So often the advances have appeared to contradict traditional Christian beliefs, and revelation from God has been thought of as incompatible with scientific discovery.

THE IMPACT OF SCIENTIFIC HUMANISM

While the honest scientist has been well enough aware of the limitations of his knowledge, there have been many ready to claim that science has all the answers and that Christian teaching is outmoded. This attitude will be considered further in a later section, but at this point it is sufficient to note that here we have the soil from which scientific humanism has so readily grown.

Contemporary **scientific humanism** presents such a rational and optimistic viewpoint, that it is easy to lose sight of the underlying assumptions which provide its driving force.

Its basic position has been succinctly described by the Rev. Alan Walker of Sydney:

> "Humanism rejects God. It claims there is no need for anything beyond man. It projects man into the place which belongs only to God. It therefore severs itself from the grace of God. Humanism lacks understanding of evil. Absurdly optimistic about human nature it opens the gates to corruption."[5]

Having identified that philosophy, we can now proceed to spell out the aspirations of humanists for social reform. The widespread pattern of change takes shape as one recognizes that it represents the efforts of humanists (among others) with clearly-defined goals. Their seven point plan is:

"1. Legalization of homosexuality between consenting males.
2. Legislation for easy abortion.
3. Legislation for easy divorce wherever the marriage has 'broken down'.
4. Legalization of euthanasia.
5. Abolition of all censorship or control of pornography.
6. Abolition of religious education in schools.
7. Permissive laws on the use of soft drugs."[6]

The fact that a substantial measure of success has already been achieved with this program should be a warning to all who hold a different philosophy of life. While plausible arguments for much of the program may be put forward and may readily attract public support, the **whole pattern** needs to be examined before parts of it are endorsed. People influenced by the prevailing teachings of situation ethics are particularly ill-equipped to offer any alternative to the humanists' program. They will readily ally themselves with much of it.

That this optimistic strain of humanism has been so influential in recent years is undeniable. But it is rather sad that humanism should be able to promote such radical changes at a time when its own underlying philosophy is being shown to be bankrupt and empty. Today, the more realistic humanists are sounding a note of despair; they are finding reality is very different from what had been supposed. Guinness has analysed these forces at some length, and notes:

> "Evolutionary optimistic humanism is in the process of being betrayed by its own idealism. . . . As with all idealism, its tragedy is the blindness of its heroes; turned into a world of illusions, they are all too vulnerable to reality . . . *[It]* is strong in its stress on the aspirations of man, but weak in its understanding of his aberrations. Accordingly, it lacks a base for the fulfilment of the former, and its solutions to the latter are deficient; thus its ultimate optimism is eternally romantic. Pessimistic humanism, on the other hand, insists on the absurdity of man's aspirations, but the price of its realism is the constant pull toward despair."[7]

Two cautionary notes must therefore be sounded. First, the social reforms being promoted with the aid of the mass media and the world of entertainment have the support or active encouragement of other significant groups in the community. Secondly, the arguments put forward to achieve reform are all too often couched in terms of scientific statements which are distorted or inaccurate. As science has become a substitute for the Bible, few question statements which come from apparent experts. It will therefore be the purpose of further chapters to illustrate the inaccuracies which are used to support an ideological position. In particular, examples will be taken relating to the arguments surrounding censorship. (See Chapter 5).

ALLIES IN SOCIAL CHANGE

Two other active groups may be identified as sympathetic to social change, though their goals may differ. The small but militant group of **radicals** and **revolutionaries** must be taken seriously since they, like the humanists, have a program to which they are dedicated. Though identified with university campuses, their sense of personal frustration and hostility against society finds a much wider echo. They align themselves with the concern of many Christians about the sick state of contemporary Western society, with its hypocritical standards and its failure to come to terms with significant human values. But their proposals for change are diametrically opposed to any Christian thinking about reconstruction or reconciliation. Whereas the Christian answer is directed to analysis of society's problems in terms of individual sin and need, the revolutionary seeks the overthrow of "the establishment" in order to make way for the "alternative society". In order to achieve such a goal, anarchy is seen as a necessary step which must be facilitated.

There are clearly-defined means for achieving the goals of overthrow of "the establishment" and creation of anarchy, though the form of the "alternative society" is less-clearly specified. However, this may be unimportant since there is ample support for those goals from **communist** influences to ensure that, at the appropriate point, conditions will be ripe for the introduction of a communist way of life. This third force, collaborating with, or at least moving in the same direction as, the other two, is producing a powerful alliance capable of infiltrating traditional values and standards over a very short space of time. In other words, while it would be clearly foolish to suggest that all the forces seeking major "permissive" reforms are communist-inspired, there are many with different motivations who are inadvertently pursuing a course which can be supported and endorsed by those openly seeking to promote communistic ideals.

Because it has been unpopular since the American McCarthy-era to identify such aspirations publicly, it is particularly important to give at least a few examples of areas where expressions of intent have been made, both in relation to revolutionary groups generally, and communists in particular.[8] These examples will be drawn only from areas relevant to the main theme of this book, and the obvious power of communism within the field of labour relations will be taken for granted.

AREAS OF ATTACK

Within the area of **sexual permissiveness**, a radical student, writing in a university newspaper, clearly expressed the goal that some are seeking:

> "We are certainly at the crossroads. So-called permissiveness, sexiness, moral relaxation have gone as far as they can without beginning to alter *radically* our civilization." *[emphasis mine]* [9]

The calculated use of sexually-explicit **entertainment** has been endorsed by the communists. In response to enquiries from party members in Italy as to how to react to it, the following was given:

> "We are interested in encouraging this type of play, and are likewise prepared to praise actors of such plays as champions of artistic freedom. We want to encourage this sort of production, and must lead people on to produce others that are, sexually speaking, more daring still. As a tactical policy our aim is to defend an enterprise which is pornographic and entirely free from the restrictions of ordinary moral rules. The producers and actors are, in effect, like ants working voluntarily and without pay for us as they eat at the very roots of bourgeois society. Why should we stop them at their work? Why should we place obstacles in their path?" [10]

The very **language** we use is the subject of attack for explicit reasons, too. Those who think the increasing acceptance of blasphemies and obscenities is simply part of an evolving contemporary society are being dangerously naive. Behind the natural developments of language associated with a fast-changing society, we need to recognize explicit encouragement of some changes rather than others.

James Michener says, "Numerous committed revolutionaries have preached that the debasement of language is one of the most powerful agencies for the destruction of existing society. They argue, 'if you destroy the word, you can destroy the system', and they have set out consciously to do both."[11]

Similarly, Richard Neville, one of the subjects of the Oz trial in London, has written that "the incidence and intensity of this 'filthy' language will increase as the new revolutionaries become less concerned with immediate issues and more determined to create total social chaos .... If anarchy is an essential precursor of the creation of an alternative society, so the deflowering of language, rendering it obscene and useless, is merely part of the process of structuring a new one."[12]

The traditional Christian restraint in use of language, including injunctions against swearing, may now be seen to have a deeper significance than was apparent in earlier times when traditional values were not being openly challenged.

The forces seeking to change **family and society** are gaining wider acceptance. A milestone of change occurred with the distribution of "The Little Red Schoolbook". This calculated indoctrination of the young was so open, and yet so skilful, that few governments saw the need to inhibit its distribution. Its title should have been enough to alert responsible authorities to its message. In spite of its direct assault on the established pattern of authority within the family and society, it has been widely distributed. Those who have tried to rationalize its acceptance as a healthy exposure of limitations in the education system must come to terms with the admission of one of the authors, who now acknowledges that the book was never intended as a comment on education, but as an exercise in anarchy.

A government that fails to restrict the influence of material of the kind found in "The Little Red Schoolbook" may be challenged in terms of the Universal Declaration of Human Rights, whose Article 16(3) states:

> "The family is the natural and fundamental group unit of society and is entitled to protection by society and the State."[13]

Similarly the terms of the UNICEF Declaration of the Rights of the Child are relevant:

> "Principle 2. The child shall enjoy special protection, and shall be given opportunities and facilities, by law and by other means, to enable him to develop physically, mentally, morally, spiritually, and socially, in a healthy and normal manner and in conditions of freedom and dignity. In the enactment of laws for this purpose, the best interests of the child shall be the paramount consideration."[14]

If an ideology is to gain maximum acceptance in the community, it will most readily do so by infiltrating the mass communication media, especially TV. That there has been a major shift in standards of acceptability in recent years is undisputed; as a result of this shift, the National Viewers' and Listeners' Association was formed in Britain.

Similar groups have sprung up in other parts of the world in reaction to the same trends in radio and TV, as well as in advertising, films, and books.

An example from TV may serve to illustrate the point. In July 1972 I accepted a request to speak on Australian national television (ABC TV) in a debate defending the proposition, "That the State should legislate in areas of personal morality". When the closing credits appeared on the screen, the final statement left with the viewer read: "That the State should **not** legislate in areas of personal morality". A mere straw in the wind, perhaps; yet less than a month later, the-then Federal Attorney-General, Senator Greenwood, was involved in an uproar over the degree of control which should be exercised over the ABC, and he stated that "a substantial group of ABC employees was trying to ensure that there would be no control over the ABC. The ideology of the group could be called 'New Left'. . . ." He referred to an article in the Communist Party publication "Tribune" of June 3, 1970, which said, "A powerful body of mass media employees are setting their sights on a struggle. . . .".

Such calculated efforts to distort information and ideas make the criterion of "prevailing community standards" a peculiarly hazardous one. This might appear to be an argument against the principle of censorship. However, it is better to see this as an argument **for** censorship properly conducted, rather than against censorship and the consequent lack of protection.

TWO CONTRIBUTING FORCES

Two other significant influences deserve mention, in view of their statements about goals which clearly influence community values. First, the development of the **liberation movements** has brought a number of ideological convictions about society in general, and the family in particular. Gay Activists press for a removal of all distinctions between homo- and hetero-sexuality, and many challenge marriage and the family as oppressive to their alternative life-style. Behind the reasonable pressures for recognition of equality of worth and opportunity (goals which no-one would wish to deny) lie strong psychological pressures to overthrow existing sex-roles.

This hostile and destructive view of society is by no means the norm for homosexuals, who generally seek to live quietly and without intrusion; the pressures for change come from the militant minority groups. So, for example, the Women's Lib journal, "Women", attacks the idea of the nuclear-family and specifically seeks its destruction.[15]

Finally, as an agent of change, the political force of **Fabian socialism** must be recognized. In lectures on this issue, the theologian, Dr. E.G. Gibson, has noted that the aims of Fabian socialism correspond to the goals of communism. The major difference between the two is that, while communism readily resorts to force to achieve its objectives, the Fabian socialist seeks to move through the processes of legislation.

Nevertheless, socialism is a force to be reckoned with, as its goals are being pursued so self-evidently. Gibson writes:

> "This [Fabian socialism] has surfaced very significantly in Dunstan and Whitlam and their various colleagues. Though Fabianism at first operated in a moderate Christian culture, today it is in a post-Christian culture and manifests all the characteristics of six abolitions: of **marriage**, of **family**, of **property**, of **education**, of **religion**, of **descent of capital**." *[emphasis mine]*[16]

It is the contention of this chapter that a pattern of change in prevailing standards is occurring. Examples of such changes have been taken from the areas of entertainment, news, the use of language, and standards of sexual morality. These changes have been identified with the aspirations of several groups, including humanists, radicals, and Communists, who should not be seen as necessarily in collaboration with each other. These groups also have in common a clear sense of purpose and a dedication to the achievement of goals, which are, in most instances, explicitly anti-Christian. These groupings, of course, should not be thought of as mutually-exclusive; for example, among humanists there are Marxists, just as there are liberationists among the Fabians.

FIGHTING FOR BETTER VALUES

Members of a democratic society cannot just call for suppression of the ideas of others in the hope that they will go away. Yet the need to inhibit the expression of ideas that will damage the society can be defended, since one important function of the law is to protect society. But more constructively, there is a real need for those who believe in Christian values to rise up to express them, defend them, proclaim them and, above all, **live** them. If among professing Christians there were a dedication to change, and a certainty about goals equal to that found among those who seek the overthrow of Christian values, there would be a very different pattern of change. We live in a society where personal responsibility for involvement is at a premium.

Happily, the indications are that recognition of this responsibility is growing in Australia and New Zealand, as well as in other parts of the world where similar forces are at work. One expression of collective Christian action has been the development of Festivals of Light in Britain, Australia, and New Zealand. This grass-roots movement will be further considered later in the book. (See Chapter 13).

5

Expert Opinion

The assertion that there is no evidence that pornography leads to criminal anti-social behaviour can be regarded as, at least, a gross exaggeration. *The Longford Report*

Behind all the ideological and political forces, we must not disregard the influence of expert opinion. Behind the elected politician is a group which evaluates evidence from all sources so that policies will be consistent with contemporary research. This situation leads one to believe that we can expect individual opinions to be tempered by sound evidence.

Yet there is reason to doubt whether the sweeping political changes we have seen in the area of censorship are based on scientifically-acceptable evidence. We are told there is no evidence that erotica is harmful to people. We are told that the violent themes in 'R' films will prove therapeutic as we face the reality of the unpleasantness of violence. We are told that, if pornography becomes freely available, people will tire of it. We are told that all these statements have a sound scientific backing.

It is by such statements that prevailing community standards are shaped. Men and women, who a few years ago would unhesitatingly have believed pornography was harmful, now speak in quite different terms. They have listened to what has been presented as expert evidence on the subject. The subtly-pervasive attitudes presented by the mass media have cumulatively been leading people to think that any objection to explicit violence or sex on the TV or cinema screen is old-fashioned or ill-informed.

We appear to be in the hands of the experts; but, in fact, the pressure is not from there at all. It is the combined resources of political pressure and financial interests which are shaping contemporary community taste.

THE CAREFUL STANCE OF EXPERTS

The experts, if there are any, would be psychologists, since their professional concern is with behaviour. The effects of external forces on attitudes and opinions are the province of psychology — and allied professions such as psychiatry and sociology. Yet it is notable that, in the debate on censorship in Australia which Mr. Chipp invited in June 1970, professionals in these fields were conspicuously slow to offer public support for the policy of liberalized censorship that he pursued. This is not to say that there is an absence of scientific studies to draw on. It is just that they are so painfully inconclusive that no scientist would retain credibility who sought to defend liberalizing policies on such grounds.

The major studies quoted by those who advocate the reduction of censorship will not stand the weight they are prepared to place upon them. Of course, the evidence is not conclusively **against** a liberalizing policy either; but it is a sound principle to make no change until there are strong grounds for change. Until we can be **sure** harm will not arise from innovations, the utmost caution should be exercised. This principle is clearly apparent in the workings of such groups as the Drug Evaluation Committee which exists to see that new drugs are not prescribed until vigorous screening has been completed. Mr. Chipp's own position in relation to marijuana followed the same principle most carefully. Against the large number of studies failing to find harm, he placed a few studies that do suggest harm. He properly stated that, as the long-term effects cannot yet be assessed, we must move cautiously for the present; once legislation permits marijuana, it will be impossible to step back.

> He is quoted as saying:
> "I have never said that marijuana is harmful. I don't know if it is. . . . Some people want marijuana legalized until it is found harmful, but this is one of the most spurious arguments I have heard."[1]

Senator Murphy, Labor's successor to Mr. Chipp, provided a most interesting parallel in his approach to French nuclear-testing in the Pacific Ocean. He took the view that some harm to future generations might arise from nuclear-testing. The evidence was greatly in dispute; but at most it appeared that some 200 people a year might suffer some physical impairment. Others were of the view that there was insufficient evidence to make a case at all. Nevertheless, on the grounds that **any** risk warranted caution, he was prepared to go and plead Australia's case at the International Court in Holland, and to register his protest in Paris directly to the French people. Consistency would demand that the same principle should apply to the possibility of psychological harm. That the evidence regarding psychological harm to children looks a great deal more convincing merely strengthens the argument.

The situation with regard to censorship is strikingly similar. The fact that large studies, including the 1970 American Presidential Commission on Obscenity and Pornography[2], failed to find evidence of harm is at best **negative** evidence. This is **not** the same as saying, "We have shown that harm will not result". It merely says, "If harm does arise, we have so far failed to find it". That Commission (which, according to some, was biased to come to such a conclusion from the start) was nevertheless properly cautious about the weight to be put on its findings, saying:

> "Analysis of the United States crime rates does not support the thesis of a causal connection between the availability of erotica and sex crimes among either juveniles or adults. Because of limitations in both the data and inferences which can validly be drawn from them, the data cannot, however, be said absolutely to disprove such a connection."

EVIDENCE OR INTERPRETATION

Scientists in this field generally are willing only to report the results of their experiments without speculation. The best reports are careful to spell out how far results can be generalized, and where the findings are of limited significance. It has remained for others less familiar with the methods of scientific investigation to make sweeping assertions.

However, in the area of *interpretation* it seems necessary for someone to say that unwarranted conclusions have been too often drawn from the data. For it is through sweeping generalizations that political changes have been made, and public attitudes have been affected. If one can show that the evidence is not really as convincing as is so often suggested, there is less reason for radical change. Indeed, with such cautionary tales available as to the effects of alcohol, tobacco, thalidomide, and DDT, we do well to ask what will be the **long-term** effects of acting on insufficient evidence.

One kind of evidence that needs to be given serious attention, if guidelines are to be set up, is that obtained from history. The taboos and laws of our own society have not evolved accidentally or without good reason. They represent the accumulated recognition that certain controls have proved desirable for the control of society. While recognizing that controls previously needed may at the present time be unnecessary, one would still need to tread cautiously before removing what may prove to be necessary provisions.

In general, it has appeared necessary to **extend** the range of legal controls as civilizations have become larger, and people have come to live in larger residential complexes. Persuasive evidence would be needed to reverse this trend in the belief that we can now do without control. The idea that man has come-of-age is attractive, but ill-substantiated. He can manage complex machinery rather better than his own emotions. Looking beyond our own culture, and examining earlier civilizations should provide evidence on different patterns of culture and their fate.

THE ARGUMENT FROM HISTORY

The idea that sexual permissiveness or licence may affect the way of life of a society has been seriously contended by various reputable writers. Much of this evidence has been summarized by Packard.[3] He draws on a variety of sociologists, anthropologists, and others, who generally share the view that permissive sexual attitudes are associated with decline in a society. Few will argue for a direct cause-and-effect link, but the strong association noted by many independent researchers needs some explanation.

J. D. Unwin is quoted by Packard as being a thorough anthropologist. His book, "Sex and Culture", published in 1934, is out-of-print and very hard to obtain, but his position may be summarized as follows: "Every civilization is established and consolidated by observing a strict sexual moral code, is maintained while this strict code is kept, . . . and decays when sexual licence is allowed. . . . Any human society is free to choose either to display great energy or to enjoy sexual freedom: the evidence is that it cannot do both for more than one generation."

Aldous Huxley has paid considerable attention to Unwin's proposition that the viability of a culture depends on the extent to which controls are exercised over sexual impulses. He describes Unwin's book as "a work of the highest importance", and, after spelling out the main conclusions that Unwin comes to, he concludes:

> "The evidence for these conclusions is so full, that it is difficult to see how they can be rejected. They are conclusions which will certainly seem unpalatable to the middle-aged relics of a liberal generation. Such liberals are liberals, not only politically, but also in the sense in which Shakespeare's 'liberal shepherds' were liberal. They have been 'heard to declare', very frequently and loudly, that they 'wish to enjoy the advantages of high culture and to abolish compulsory continence'. Living as they do upon the capital of energy accumulated by a previous generation of monogamists, whose wives came to them as *virgines intactae,* they can make the best of both worlds during their own life-time. Dr. Unwin's researches have made it certain, however, that it will be impossible for their children to go on making the best of both worlds."[4]

Not everyone, however, is persuaded of the quality of Unwin's studies or his conclusions; so Packard helpfully cites the opinion of Dr. David Mace, who was a fellow-student with Unwin. Mace says, "His work was flamboyant on a colossal scale . . . I think there is something fundamentally sound about his general position".

In a series of lectures delivered to students at Oxford, Professor V.A. Demant[5] has drawn on Unwin's views in defending the case for cultures remaining strong when sexual desires are kept under constraint. He also draws on numerous other writers, many of them not writing from a Christian position. In particular, he quotes extensively from Kardiner's book, "Sex and Morality", to substantiate Unwin's views. Packard also refers to several other writers, among whom notably are the sociologist Zimmerman and the historian Toynbee, "who have offered strong cautionary evidence about the hazards of sexual permissiveness". In so far as these men work within their own areas of competence, their views must be seriously considered.

FROM THE RECENT PAST

The other major scientist who has documented evidence in this area is the Harvard sociologist, Professor Pitrim Sorokin. Moving from Eastern Europe to America, he noticed striking parallels in America to what he had seen around the time of the Russian Revolution. A great deal of statistical data is contained in his "Sociology of Revolution"[6]; in "The American Sex Revolution", his analysis of trends in sexual morality has a ring of uncomfortable familiarity:

> "During the first stage of the Revolution, its leaders deliberately attempted to destroy marriage and the family. Free love was glorified by the official 'glass of water' theory: if a person is thirsty, so went the Party line, it is immaterial what glass he uses when satisfying his thirst; it is equally unimportant how he satisfies his sex hunger. The legal distinction between marriage and casual sexual intercourse was abolished. The communist law spoke only of 'contracts' between males and females for the satisfaction of their desires either for an indefinite or definite period — a year, a month, a week, or even a single night. One could marry and divorce as many times as desired. Husband or wife could obtain a divorce without the other being notified. Bigamy, and even polygamy, were permissible under the new provisions. Abortion was facilitated in State institutions. Pre-marital relations were praised, and extra-marital relations were considered normal.
>
> "Within a few years, hordes of wild, homeless children became a real menace to the Soviet Union itself. Millions of lives, especially of young girls, were wrecked; divorces skyrocketed, as also did abortions. The hatreds and conflicts among polygamous and polyandrous mates rapidly mounted — and so did psycho-neurosis. Work in the nationalized factories slackened.
>
> "The total results were so appalling that the Government was forced to reverse its policy. The propaganda of 'the glass of water' theory was declared to be counter-revolutionary, and its place was taken by official glorification of pre-marital chastity and of the sanctity of marriage. Abortion was prohibited except, since 1945, in exceptional conditions involving the health of the mother or similar considerations. The liberty of divorce was radically curtailed; by the decree of July 1944, it was made impossible for the vast majority of citizens. By now the cycle has been completed, and a slight relaxation of this too-severe repression of sex is making it moderately normal. Soviet Russia today has a more monogamic, stable, and Victorian family and marriage life than most of the Western countries.
>
> "Considering that the wide cycle occurred under a single regime, the experiment is highly informative. It clearly shows the destructive consequences of unlimited sex freedom, especially in regard to creative growth."[7]

Here again, one may ask whether Sorokin is a reliable source. His international reputation is such that in 1963 a book was published[8] containing evaluations of his work by experts from around the world. David Mace was called upon to evaluate his theories on sex and society. His critique is a careful one; he states:

> "Sorokin's thesis is that irregularities of sexual behaviour are personally and socially deleterious. In general, I am in agreement with him. The libertine, the profligate, the fornicator, the adulterer, the seducer: these are, in consequence of their sexual acts, disturbers and destroyers of the health and security of the body social. The interests of family and community alike are best served by adherence to the traditional standards of chastity and fidelity which have, in their highest periods of achievement, characterized the great human cultures."

Against such a background, we find statements often made in the name of science which suggest that little harm will arise from declining standards. When we turn to the evidence on which such claims are based, it proves to be a great deal more fragile than at first appears. A few of the better-known and most-commonly-used studies will serve as examples.

CURRENT CLAIMS ON PORNOGRAPHY

1. The studies of B. Kutschinsky have been widely used in support of the view that erotica is not harmful. His study on the effects of pornography[9] was prepared for the American Presidential Commission, and has since been published separately. The general interpretation of this study is that people become less interested in pornography as a result of viewing it, and less interested also in engaging in sexually-deviate behaviour. These are indeed the broad conclusions of the paper, and hold true for the majority of subjects tested (72 university students of both sexes).

However, usefulness of the study must be tempered by the following information derived from the report itself. It was described as "a pilot experiment" and "exploratory study". The subjects "were somewhat more experienced with pornography than the average population of Copenhagen. . . The fact that the subjects volunteered for the experiment and did not get any payment is reason enough to call for caution in making generalizations from the findings in such a study." That the material was presented to the whole group simultaneously rather than individually may also have affected results; the study notes that the pornography "quickly became boring, disappointing and uniform — at least when viewed in public and passivity . . . Part of the reason for this apparent lack of public success might be that pornography is, in fact, not made for public viewing but for private use".

In discussing the results, Kutschinsky cautions, "We shall not try to discuss the extent to which these findings can be generalized to abnormal persons, non-students, non-Danes, exposure in privacy, and completely different types of pornography. Whether expected or not, most of these findings have in common that they cannot be considered confirmed in this study. This means, among others, that they are unsuitable as a basis for a serious debate on the political level".

2. The view that sex crimes go down following the introduction of pornography is canvassed widely. It is clear that most, who so proudly use this as an argument for pornography, are quite unfamiliar with the original source. If they really knew the original material, they would be embarrassed to mention the study, because it can be used to support this proposition only by the most devious sophistry. The evidence is to be found in Kutschinsky's report entitled, "Towards an explanation of the decrease in registered sex crimes in Copenhagen". It shows a decrease of 63% in registered heterosexual crimes over the ten-year period 1959-1969.

Accepting these figures as correct, the important issue is what they mean. Over against the simple interpretation so commonly given, the following must be set:

(i) The study relates to Copenhagen, which has such a different cultural background from Australian cities, that it is unwise to compare too readily;

(ii) The noted decline related to **minor** sex offences;

(iii) The noted decline related to heterosexual offences, and gave no information regarding homosexual offences;

(iv) Some of the drop (particularly relating to exhibitionism and indecency towards women) arises from a decreased readiness to report (overall about 17%);

(v) While written pornography was legalized in 1967, the decline was occurring long before this. The study goes back to 1959, and while one may say that much pornography was circulating illicitly then, this antedating (and absence of comparable evidence before then) makes the argument for legalization weak.

OTHER FACTORS IN THE DANISH CASE

All the preceding points arise directly from the study itself. In addition, however, there are further considerations:

(vi) A more recent report from Denmark has stated that "sexual offences reported to the police are now predominantly serious and violent. Rape, and assault-and-battery connected with sadism, are more common. Crimes of this nature have risen by about 5% since 1969".[10] Since that report, statistics have revealed that the incidence of reported rape and attempted-rape had risen from 27 cases in 1969 to 63 in 1972.

(vii) Mary Whitehouse, following discussion with Kutschinsky, concluded that although the laws relating to heterosexual offences are unchanged, police attitudes to intervention have become more lenient.[11] In this context, Gummer has written:

> "Closer examination has revealed that the drop in sex crimes was apparent rather than real. At the same time as the pornography law was changed, a number of activities which had previously

been illegal became legal. The manufacture, selling, and advertising of pornography, voyeurism, and similar offences were all abolished; so, as there were fewer crimes on the Statute Book, the number of crimes dropped."

"No doubt", he adds acidly, "if burglary were made legal, the Copenhagen crime rate would fall still further."[12]

(viii) The drop in offences does not mean that people's sexual problems have been solved by pornography. Equally, one may say that the deviate has simply exchanged one activity for another, which, for a time, involves fewer offences against others. Data relating to offences against children since 1970 indicate that here, too, a rise in frequency occurred beyond what had been known for a long time.

During a personal visit by the author to Copenhagen in 1974, it was possible to establish with the police department that a series of significant changes in the law **has** occurred, influencing not only actual reporting-levels, but also the climate of opinion in the community relating to sexual behaviour. In particular, 11 paragraphs, which had previously been included in statistics, were altered or liberalized in August 1967. Some categories, which had previously included substantial figures, were reduced to nil (for example, homosexual prostitution). R. Ben-Veniste, in his report to the American Commission, considered the question of reporting-changes in the law, and the relation of these to the actual incidence of offences. He considered that there might well be a real drop in minor sex offences, but that this did not apply to the more serious offences like rape. These, he said, "are probably not diminished statistically by changes in attitude towards reporting, or at least to the same extent as with minor offences, by the ability of hard-core pornography to channel potentially-deviant behaviour into inoffensive auto-eroticism."13

This clear recognition of possible links between pornography and sexual offences is worth noting, since so many critics seek to suggest that no such link can be established. Or, more exactly, the link is acknowledged when a **decline** in offences occurs, but it is rejected as spurious when an **increase** occurs. Explanations must not be simplistically related to changes either way; but consistency does demand an honest appraisal of figures in both directions.

(ix) A most important omission from the studies of both Ben-Veniste and Kutschinsky is reference to the base-rate population in Copenhagen. For the numbers of offences to be correctly interpreted, they should have been reported as a rate (offences per 100,000 of population) to take into account changes in the number of people at risk over the period of study. They should have noted two unusual features of the Copenhagen population. First, the total numbers have been steadily declining, from a peak of 768,105 in 1950 to 605,639 in 1972. This decline, associated with city rebuilding, is sociologically significant. Secondly, the population that remains tends to be much older than the average for the country as a whole, for the younger people are moving out to the suburbs. Therefore the group most likely to commit sexual offences is greatly reduced in numbers within the area of Copenhagen covered by the figures discussed by Kutschinsky and Ben-Veniste.

THE TREND IN STATISTICS

(x) We cannot know in advance what will be the long-term changes in a society with freely-available pornography, or whether those who use it will tire of it and turn again to offences against others. Gummer says:

> "The regular exposition of pornographic material, and the general abuse heaped upon anyone who seeks to oppose it, has lessened considerably the willingness of the ordinary person to complain even of those activities which are still illegal. People who can go and watch group-sex activities of the most perverted kind are not very likely to complain about possible prostitution over the way. It would hardly be surprising if the figures for sex crimes reported to the police did not fall, and the fact that in the major sectors there has been no such drop may indicate an **increase** in crimes." *[emphasis mine]* 14

An interesting parallel may now be observed in Britain, where, with relaxed censorship restrictions, it appeared that sex crimes might be reduced. For the first half of 1972, Scotland Yard's figures indicate an increase in crimes of violence (including wounding and assault), as well as in rape, robbery, fraud, and shoplifting.

Rape cases recorded increased by 50%, from 48 during the first half of 1971, to 72 in the first half of 1972. The "Daily Telegraph" said of this:

> "This follows the downward trend of last year. There had been a decrease in sexual offences for several years, but the situation has now swung around. The fact that there has been such a heavy increase in the recorded cases gives rise to concern that the 'hidden number' of sexual offences generally may be soaring."

Allowing that year-by-year analyses of crimes can often be misleading, the Scotland Yard figures for London over a longer period of time call for study. The trend with relation to rape is unmistakable. The Police Commissioner's Reports reveal that the average level of reported cases for the five years 1964-1968 was 64.6, while the average for the five years 1969-1973 was 124.8. Increases far outstripping population-growth appear to have been occurring since the early 60s. These rises must be seen in the perspective of other types of crime. Often it is plausibly suggested by those unfamiliar with the evidence that rises in sexual crimes are just part of a general trend of increased crime in society. In many places, it is true, marked rises in other kinds of crimes are also occurring, but the rises are small compared with the figures cited above. The most effective contrast may be made with recent British figures. In England and Wales, crime **fell** by 3.8% in the period January-September 1973.15 This was the biggest decline for some years. Yet in that same period, offences of violence **rose** by 19.3%, and sexual offences **rose** by 11.5%. Clearly, these problems are more than just another symptom of a sick society; the relatively-greater increase suggests that something additional is at work. A similar pattern, with increases in rape reports going far beyond the trends for other crimes, is apparent in police statistics for 1973-74 in Victoria and South Australia.

(xi) Those who give credence to Kutschinsky's findings would do well to note that the Danish Minister for Justice, in writing to the Longford Commission, said "Berl Kutschinsky issued his report in 1970 . . . He stressed that his findings were temporary".[16]

EVALUATING SCIENTIFIC TESTS

3. Another much-quoted study, also conducted for the American Commission, was a laboratory study of exposure to pornography. This study, by C.B. Reifler *et al*, has been taken as convincing evidence that when pornography becomes freely available, satiation will occur and demand will drop. It involved getting 23 male students to spend 90 minutes a day for three weeks looking at pornographic materials. At the end of this time the students showed decreased interest in, and response to, pornography. To understand the limitations of this study, let the authors speak for themselves:

> "Several qualifications must be placed on the conclusions presented in this report. Our subjects were young, white adults, whose educational level and socio-economic background is greater than the national average. . . Given the opportunity to withdraw, eighteen of the seventy initial volunteers withdrew. . . The fact that these subjects were self-selected is not as worrisome in terms of potential generalizability as is their age and educational level . . . Most exposures to pornography do not, however, occur under the solitary conditions of social isolation that were part of the design of this experiment. We do not know what effects on response to pornography would be, if additional variables of social interaction with individuals or groups, of the same sex, or opposite sex, were added. Can our findings be generalized to younger, less-well-educated, or less stable populations? In order to be certain, additional studies would have to be done . . ."[17]

Over against these negative results, one must place a good and more recent experiment by G. Schmidt and V. Sigusch.[18] They presented erotic material to men and women, using films and slides so that viewing was conducted alone for only 10 minutes. Subjects were asked to respond to questions about the sexually-arousing nature of the situation, but also about their more general feelings. Although the experiment was brief, both sexes showed strong emotional reactions. Men said they became bored, aggressive, gregarious, excited, wild, cheered up, emotional, and agitated. Women showed a greater adverse reaction, and added that they also felt shocked, driven, jumpy, disgusted, irritated, angered, and numb. Women differed from the men in not feeling more gregarious or cheered up. Since the experimental situation was much more realistic than the 22.5 hours of satiation by Reifler, these reactions probably give a fairer indication of the effects of erotica under usual viewing conditions.

4. Another of the Kutschinsky studies[19] has been used to demonstrate that demand for pornography in Denmark has dropped dramatically since it became legitimate. This paper's findings were discussed critically in "No, No, Calcutta", where I said:

> "It is true that the evidence shows reduced income for the producers and that some have gone out of business. It is also true that the tourists buy more than the locals. Does this prove the point? On the contrary — for several reasons. The figures indicating reduced demand relate to the amount of money spent, not the number of items purchased. With legalization, the cost of books was reduced by around 50 per cent. Thus to maintain the appearance of equal demand, twice the number of items would have to be sold. With this new economic structure, many of the small producers dropped out, leaving the business in the hands of bigger and better-organized concerns. Furthermore, the extent to which books are passed around undoubtedly changes following legalization. With censorship, a banned book has a limited audience; if legitimate, it will become available to many readers — and correspondingly have a tendency to reduce sales.
>
> "It is also worth noting what is sold today in Denmark. When only written pornography was made available, that of course formed the market. With the introduction of pictorial material in 1969, this began to take over. The availability of pornographic films and live sex shows must be reckoned with, too. There has been a large reduction in sales of written pornography (now accounting for only 5 per cent of the market) while pictorial material (over 50 per cent) and sexual 'objects' have taken over a large part of the market.
>
> "This shift of interest to more and more realistic aids to fantasy makes clear that evidence of reduced sales of literature is only one part of the story. Such increasing approximations to involvement in sexual perversions must eventually lead away from the vicarious experience to a demand for more personal involvement in them. Such a trend also makes clear that discussion of literary merit is largely irrelevant to what would happen if censorship were abolished in this country.
>
> "The Kutschinsky study of customers in porno shops in Copenhagen showed that a high proportion (25%) were probably foreigners, and they bought disproportionately more than residents. One must nevertheless account for 75% of local customers who come to browse but not to buy. We may reasonably argue that while the foreigner must buy to ensure continued availability of material, the residents who find themselves able to obtain a little-but-often contact free by browsing will scarcely bother to buy. Such lines of argument strongly discount the proposition that legalization makes pornography less attractive."[20]

ANOTHER VOICE FROM DENMARK

More recently, a closely-similar interpretation regarding changing tastes has appeared in "The Little White Book", originally printed in Denmark:

"Pornography is not just a matter of innocent people trying to earn their living by selling some dirty pictures. Pornography is a vast industry. Greedy money-makers are behind it. The Bible speaks about them: 'They have eyes for nothing but women, eyes which never rest from sin . . . masters in mercenary greed, God's curse is on them!

"You have probably heard Denmark mentioned in connection with pornography. The writers of this little book are Danish, too! And we should like to make clear what is the real state of affairs in our country, which we love. Many Danes do not like pornography. It has been inflicted on them by a minority who, before anybody could realize what was going on, flooded Denmark with a tidal wave of filth.

"We will describe the process step by step so that you can learn from our experiences and not be ensnared as we were. . . The same evil forces are at work in your country. Things began to escalate in Denmark back in 1967. At that time people wanted written pornography to be freed from censorship. Consequently there was heavy pressure on the law against pornographic literature. In those critical days the Supreme Court could not really decide what was 'art' and what was 'pornography' — so pornography in print was let loose.

"It was claimed that when the forbidden fruit was no longer forbidden, it would die. And that philosophy was right — to a certain extent. Some reduction in sales of porn books was noted. But pornography itself did not die. On the contrary, a chain reaction started. Lust turned to stronger stuff. Pornography changed its direction and concentrated on obscene pictures. People could no longer be satisfied by reading mere words of pornography (which was now unrestricted) — they wanted to see pictures. Again there was heavy pressure on the law, and the Government decided to allow pictures uncensored.

"But pornography still did not die. The insatiable lust of man turned to new realms. People could no longer be satisfied by seeing pictures (which were now unrestricted); they wanted to see porn in action in films. Yet again, this heavy pressure on the law, and the decision was made to remove all censorship on films. This has influenced the whole Danish film industry — and this in its turn has had a certain influence on television. Then it was no longer satisfying to see porn on films (which were now unrestricted) — people wanted to see the real thing done in front of them by living human beings on a stage.

> "So we got the so-called 'live shows' which, of course, are really the new name for centres of prostitution. These have developed into disgusting places of cruelty and bestiality and performances which we will not mention here. But lust knows no bounds until it reaches the final destruction of human dignity. And when it's impossible to think of more methods of defiling man — these forces will throw off their mask. Their ultimate effect is to defile the holy things of God."[21]

This prediction, that the pornographers would in due course turn to blasphemy, has now been thoroughly confirmed. Films such as "The Devils" are increasing in number, marked not only by destructive attacks on Christian themes, but also by glorification of all that is evil.

In Denmark in 1973, publicity was given to the intention to make a film about the love-life of Jesus Christ. The plot was clearly a monstrous perversion of the truth, yet the film-makers were to be Government-subsidized. However, contrary to the libertarian view that all Danes now accept this kind of thing calmly, the fact is that a petition with 147,000 signatures resulted in a change of policy and the withdrawal of the promised subsidy. A Gallup Poll revealed that, even in Denmark, 76% disapproved of the Government funding, and 62% considered the film should be forbidden. Here is one further indication that, even in Denmark, the forces for good are far greater in numbers than that destructive but dedicated minority who promote corruption in the name of freedom.

CURRENT STANCES ON VIOLENCE

5. Regarding the possible impact of violence on people's attitudes and behaviour, there has been less disagreement; but here, too, it is revealing to see the message which is reaching the community to shape its standards. In Mr. Chipp's ministerial statement of June 1970, he said:

> "The findings of the Eisenhower Commission on the Causes and Prevention of Violence are significant. Referring to violence in television programs, the Commission states that it is reasonable to conclude that a constant diet of violence has an adverse effect on the human character and attitudes. Television violence is a contributing factor to violence in society."

What then of the still-more-powerful film projected at the theatre or drive-in? The introduction of the 'R' classification has made a new breed of films available, some of which explore violence more deeply than ever before. "Straw Dogs" may be cited as a case in point. It is argued that the restricted nature of the showings makes such releases acceptable. This might be so if one could assume the films were viewed only by mature and balanced audiences; but the prevalence of disturbed adults who are able to view such films is uncomfortably high. Recognizing that more people with psychiatric illnesses are outside hospitals than in, can we afford to ignore the impact on such people?

Further, it is often argued that "you don't have to go to see them if you don't want to". Against this, it must be said that the impact is not restricted to the viewer alone. In this connection, James Wall has recently written:

> "Someone may object that, despite the power of film, it is still a matter that one can take or leave as one chooses, that film exercises an influence only on those who attend movies. We must be well aware that a cultural medium, with the potency that film has, exercises an impact far beyond the immediate viewing. From superficial things such as clothing styles to profound social attitudes, film affects the public. . . The image of the black man in American films was not only influenced by the pattern of American racism that is causing the nation so much grief today, but it also helped to establish that pattern. . . And the non-film-going public experiences these changes without ever visiting a theatre."[22]

Other views are sometimes publicly expressed. In a newspaper discussion of the workings of the 'R' certificate system, an expert was quoted as saying that the portrayal of unadulterated violence might prove therapeutic to viewers.

Such an argument if backed by scientific evidence would be persuasive. The average reader cannot be blamed if he assumes that the expert cited was correct, as well as being correctly quoted. In fact, both assumptions proved incorrect. Believing the best and most recent evidence [23, 24] to suggest that people will readily imitate violence if it is viewed without any indication that it must be curbed, the statements made were questioned in correspondence. Once again, the careful expert's actual position emerged from behind the speculative generalization of the press:

> "The so-called 'Feshbach hypothesis' suggested that an angry subject would have his tendencies towards violence reduced after viewing a violent film, and his paper certainly seemed to support this notion. In fact, I have always been very suspicious about this, and in more recent years there have been a series of papers which tend to come to the opposite conclusion."[25]

THE ROLE OF THE PRESS

That same letter concluded with a thoughtful observation about the available scientific evidence. "I assess it justifies a reasonably cautious stance. In ordinary discussion, of course, strong viewpoints are expressed on political or ideological grounds rather than on the basis of what relatively little evidence we have."

It is interesting to speculate why the press will present the opposite view to that which the expert believes. Certainly it makes a travesty of trying to apply prevailing community standards as a criterion for censorship, since it is through the press that so many opinions are moulded.

One major reason for distortions in the press is the humanistic philosophy which is projected. This results, in spite of all protestations to the contrary, in a highly-biased selection of news and comment. Views contrary to humanism are commonly omitted, and thereby the very worst kind of censorship is being exercised.

This bias has repeatedly occurred in the press, with the catharsis theory being used to promote the beneficial effects of pornography and the like. "Catharsis" (literally, *cleansing*) is the term which is used to refer to the idea that a significant emotional experience (for example, through viewing violence, or being exposed to pornography) can act as a safety-valve which prevents uncontrolled acts and expressions of feeling. Thus, in a national newspaper, in an article about the effects of viewing violence, a criminologist with a humanistic viewpoint said, "There are cases which can show people who find their need for excitement vicariously satisfied by watching these things on film". A letter from the author, asking for evidence to support this statement, brought a reply that **no evidence could be offered.** Such humanistic speculations demand stronger foundations — especially when they are repeated with such confidence.

EVIDENCE FOR THE VERY OPPOSITE

In fact, the present evidence goes rather the other way. The whole catharsis theory has been examined by Liebert and his colleagues and found wanting. They criticize the original work which gave rise to the idea, and go on to show that more recent experiments have produced results more consistent with the idea that people will imitate what they see, at least under certain conditions. They refer to the Surgeon General's summary of a study by Wells which said, among other things:

> ". . . in a direct reversal of Feshbach and Singer — Wells found significantly greater physical aggressiveness among boys who viewed the more violent television programs . . . the differences were limited to boys who were above average in aggression before the study began."

They cite a further study which found "no evidence for catharsis . . . in naturally occurring aggressive behaviour; instead, exposure to entertainment violence instigated more aggression than was found among boys who watched non-aggressive fare", and then conclude:

> "the data suggest a possibility **directly opposite** to the catharsis hypothesis — that watching aggression may have an **instigating** effect on the observer, making him **more** likely to be aggressive." *[emphasis mine]* [26]

This chapter has so far indicated that evidence from cultures in the past does show that a real danger exists in getting away from moral standards. While we would expect evidence in our own time to confirm this, a great deal has been said to suggest that we have nothing to fear. It has therefore been shown that there are major objections to an unquestioning acceptance of that claim. It is not good enough just to make the point.

Having said that, it is necessary to put forward evidence to make the case that there **are** real dangers. In addition, one needs to answer a reasonable criticism that the evidence discussed here is one-sided or deliberately biased. This objection can be best answered briefly at this point by drawing on a particularly-thorough review of the evidence by Professor Eysenck, who is at pains not to take sides. He discusses the arguments and evidence dispassionately, and then states:

> "I think the evidence shows fairly conclusively . . . that pornographic writings and pictures do have a definite effect in shifting the average person's behaviour . . . it seems only too likely that the changes that have taken place have indeed increased sexual depravity . . . if they [anti-censorship advocates] argue in terms of lack of proof for the 'tendency to deprave and corrupt', as many have done in the past, then it is to be feared that their arguments receive very little support from experimental psychology."[27]

That reaction is more recent and more valuable than the bland denial of harm offered by those whose study stopped with the American Presidential Report of 1970. Some of the more solid indications of harm associated with pornography, explicit sex, and excessive violence, have alreay been introduced in these chapters; the evidence bearing on pornography will be summarized below in Chapter 7.

6

The Importance of Viewpoint

The future of our society demands that it be protected against the expansion of an unbridled sexuality which is brought about on a massive scale by the products of a powerful and unscrupulous industry.

Pope Paul VI

The examples of the previous chapter serve as illustrations of the general proposition that there is a "credibility gap" between the scientific evidence on the one hand, and public statements and opinions on the other. Since scientific studies do not appear to be adequate to justify the relaxation of censorship that has been undertaken, and since, moreover, public opinion apparently lags behind the changes that film producers and publishers are seeking to introduce, an explanation for the discrepancies should be sought.

The most obvious explanations come readily to hand. On the one hand, the expert adviser has a professional reputation at stake, and will not commit himself beyond the data. Consequently, very few scientists are prepared to make public statements on an issue like censorship when the data are still unclear. By contrast, publishers and producers, together with the mass media, have a big financial interest in gaining the freedom to deal with themes in a new way. To break through society's taboos and to shock the audience is certain to provide an income.

Michael Boddy, the theatre writer of "The Bulletin", has written: "Prurience and a heated involvement with sexuality is the very stuff of journalism; but in my job I handle a hundred or more press-cuttings a week about live theatre, and I've noticed recently that even in this restricted field 85% of the cuttings are obsessed in some way with sex and shock. The stuff has become a cancer. The sole interest a reporter or columnist seems to have in a show is the probable sexuality, or the possible shock-content. No-one ever asks whether the show is to be any good, or whether people will have a good time when they see it. He will ask, though, whether people will be shocked. This single-mindedness is appalling." In such a situation it takes people of conscience to ask whether the long-term effects on society may be detrimental.

CHANGE IS NEVER STATIC

It follows, of course, that standards must be constantly revised as the previously-shocking material becomes commonplace. Contemporary community standards, therefore, become a prey for the publisher who wishes to exploit change for his own advantage. Under these circumstances, there is only one possible direction of change.

> "What shocks an audience today will be acceptable tomorrow, and thus the contemporary dramatist is constantly impelled to seek further excesses to gratify a warped taste which he himself implanted in the public mind."[1]

At the present time the indications are that this change is self-perpetuating, and being fostered by those who can capitalize from it. Raymond Gauer has written of the American scene:

> "Not only do misleading articles about 'passing porno fads' lull many into a false sense of complacency, i.e., 'pornography is killing itself off' — but the saturation of our society by pornography creates a vicious circle that discourages and frustrates those who are concerned. For example, the producers of the "Dean Martin Show" can say, 'How can you object to Dean's lecherous comments and *double entendre* jokes, when you've got books like "The Sensuous Woman" in your libraries?' To those who object to such material in libraries the defence will point to pornographic films being screened at local drive-ins. Those who object to that are referred to the peep-show arcades and skin-flick storefront theatres that many communities now 'tolerate' on the basis that, compared to live sex shows, they are not so bad, etc., etc., etc. What happens is that the lowest form of pornography 'tolerated' by a community becomes the yardstick against which all other forms of community morality are measured. This sad but true fact highlights the wisdom of the original drafters of obscenity laws who rightly pointed out that such laws are essential in order to protect the public morality."[2]

In addition to those who are using exploitation for financial advantage, it is necessary to take account of others pushing in the same direction for ideological reasons. It is no longer a matter for doubt that the radicals who seek the overthrow of our society are pushing hard for the acceptance of pornography. "The Little Red School Book" gives extensive coverage to the familiar themes of drugs, sex, and violence. The aim of that book, as admitted by one of the authors, is not education but anarchy. Predictably, children are advised to try out the ideas that they encounter when they see pornography. Both the title of that book and its contents identify its Maoist associations.

The approach is not new, but entirely consistent with the following, attributed to Joseph Stalin: "By making readily available drugs of various kinds, by giving a teenager alcohol, by praising his wildness, by strangling him with sex literature and advertising [directed] to him or her, this psychopolitical preparation can create the necessary attitude of chaos, idleness, and worthlessness, into which can then be cast the solution which will give the teenager complete freedom everywhere. If we can effectively kill the national pride and patriotism of just one generation we will have won that country. Therefore, there must be continued propaganda abroad to undermine the loyalty of the citizens in general, and the teenager in particular."[3]

NEW AWARENESS IS NEEDED

Unfortunately, many who ought to be alert to the dangers under-estimate them. Because pornography is thought to be something cheap and trashy, it is disregarded and treated as if it were beneath the notice of the responsible citizen. It is becoming increasingly necessary to emphasize that pornography can take many forms, including the sophisticated presentation of a philosophy of life which closely associates pornography with atheism. So Francis Schaeffer says:

> "There have always been pornographic writings, but the new ones are different. They are not just dirty writings of the kind that were always available — many of today's pornographic works are philosophic statements. . . The fantastic thing is that . . . they are writing pornographic material today in the hope that finally an ethic for the golden age will drop out. They conceive of pornography as the ultimate release — it is the leap to freedom. And although there is, of course, much trash as well, there is in these serious pornographic writings, struggling with this problem, the hope that pornography will provide a new golden age. . . These people are in total desperation. We are fighting for our lives. If we love men, this is no age for a lack of comprehension."[4]

Something of the danger to society that pornography poses has now been recognized even by the writer Max Harris. A visit to Europe several years ago appears to have made a significant change in his attitudes. While he says, "I am and always shall be anti-censorship", he hastens to add, "But I do confess that there is a dire problem of pornography; that the young are threatened by it; that it is being crudely and ruthlessly promoted. . . Society is building the pornographic or infantile psychology into the framework of accepted values and behaviour patterns. The young are educating themselves into the idea of sex as a personal appetite — to be evaluated and indulged as such. . . This is the modern agony of the young. This is the most radically destructive force that has happened to the Western human psyche over the past two revolutionary decades".[5]

Also commenting on those who are behind the move to change the standards of acceptability, Gummer says, "What is absolutely clear is that drug-culture, pornography, and extreme radicalism are usually found together, and nowhere so obviously as in the world of publishing". This has the support of the intellectual elite minority who see permissiveness as an important step in the creation of a more tolerant society, and "they want it because it provides a sort of equality of opportunity in vice. Then there is the broad mass of young people who have had the opportunity to create it. Beyond them both are the apostles of disorder for whom permissiveness in sex and drugs is merely part of a new permissiveness which would replace order with continual revolution, and bring us to a violent society in which no value will be safe and no person".[6]

In Australia similarly, there are the indications that a vocal minority is seeking major changes, the outcome of which is at best uncertain. Here Professor D. Maddison can be quoted:

> "The society that the majority of people have wanted up till very recent times has decreed, for example, that the public exhibition of sexual intercourse would be a spectacle reserved for the definitely kinky, vigorously suppressed by the law and by public opinion. If we wish to change all this, and though it is only a minority at present who might wish to see such a change, they are a very vocal minority indeed (and they obtain the raucous support of the popular press), then we need to be clear what we are doing, and clear that the result will be a society different in fundamental, and somewhat unpredictable, ways from the one we know now. Despite those who feel that all change must inevitably be for good, the possible repercussions are enormous and by no means easily categorized or foreseen — repercussions on child development, on the structure of the family, on the utilization of certain amounts of sexual energy for non-sexual purposes, and so on."[7]

A VOICE IS RAISED

Since in this debate the question of who constitutes a majority is a recurrent one, a piece of local evidence is also worth a mention. In South Australia, two major petitions have been presented to State Parliament during the last few years relating to the issues under consideration. The first asked that the stage presentation of "Oh! Calcutta!" should be restrained. Although many saw such a petition as negative, and felt unable to sign without first seeing the revue, over 20,000 signatures were obtained. Those who took the opposite view sought to offset this with a counter-petition. The result was 5,300 signatures.

Actual numbers like this do not prove anything; but, if the majority really does want freedom from restraint, it is hard to explain the relatively poor response to the counter-petition.

Similarly, more recently, petitions were circulated seeking the control of sex shops. Again, many thousands of signatures were obtained. The response was such that a self styled Moral Freedom Committee publicly announced a counter-petition. Once more, the accumulation of support for no restraints fell far short. This is remarkable since it is generally more popular to be *for* something than *against*.

Further support for the view that the majority really want decency has been seen in both Britain and America. When a National Petition for Decency was circulated in Britain, 85% of those asked to sign were willing to do so. In some areas (where samples were carefully checked), over 90% gave their support. The result was the collection of 1,350,000 signatures, the biggest petition ever presented to the British Parliament. This degree of support corresponds closely to the Gallup Poll 85% support for censorship reported in America in the Obscenity Commission report.

The whole matter was taken very seriously by a combined churches study carried out in Tamworth, New South Wales, in 1975. A total of 3,993 people of the area was asked a series of questions on censorship and the data were computer-processed. To the question "Do you believe there is need for some form of censorship for books, magazines, and films?", 90% (3,600) said "Yes". Father LeFevre, the parish priest of South Tamworth, said that such massive support for "some form of censorship" showed that the people of the area did not want pornographic and obscene literature readily available in the community. Most questions were deliberately broad, but one precise question was asked, viz., "Do you favour clear enforcement laws against the production and distribution of obscene publications and films?". To this, 88% (3,511) said "Yes". This study, predictably, received little attention in the national press.

That there is so great a groundswell of support is a surprise to politicians and the media alike. No doubt this is so because the libertarians have previously enjoyed an advantage by being more active and better organized, and more willing to use aggressive tactics which the supporters of decency refuse to adopt.

A FAIR HEARING FOR ALL

At the most fundamental level, the question of who has the majority is irrelevant. Even if the supporters of decency were only a tiny minority, their view should still be heard, along with others, and receive serious attention. We do not seek to impose our view on others, but we do insist that our view should be given a fair hearing. There are indications that this is now being recognized at government level and in the media. But it requires continued energy and clarity of expression to earn continued attention. Being vaguely well-intentioned, but lacking a clearly thought-out position, very properly means that public opportunities to be heard will not become available.

It is, for example, not good enough simply to dismiss pornography with emotive adjectives like "trashy", "filthy", etc. Given freedom to develop, pornography has in places become sophisticated and glossy.

It is, in part, just because of this that we must view recent developments in censorship as highly dangerous to the community.

The move to introduce 'R' books confirmed Mr. Chipp's intention to proceed with a "liberalizing" policy far beyond what the community seeks. There can be no evidence that community standards are such that an additional range of books should be made available. Once again it is the arrogant assumption that, because an intellectual elite want restricted material made available, they must be satisfied. The proposal is made to appear attractive by referring to books of "high literary, sociological, or historical merit".

A similar argument was advanced for the 'R' film. It is therefore necessary to repeat that **a defence on the basis of literary or artistic merit is irrelevant if material is unacceptable on other grounds.** Both pro- and anti-censorship parties will agree about that. The view that high quality may even make themes more dangerous has been well-illustrated by the release of "The Devils" — a film of undoubted artistic merit, but, because of this, the more disturbing to those who view it. The disastrous consequences of "A Clockwork Orange" undoubtedly arose not only because of the content of the film, but also because the quality of production was so high.

QUO VADIS?

Looking to the future, we now await the release of the film "Manson" — a portrayal of the grisly combination of sex, drugs, occult, and murder, which originally shocked the world. A British film reviewer seeing this film at a Film Festival said, "This film is brilliant. I say it must never be released in Britain."[8] The British Board of Film Censors has wisely followed that advice; yet, tragically, the Greater London Council has decided to allow it to screen in London. This technically-excellent production could well bring some re-enactments in real life.

What Mr. Chipp initiated in this field was taken up by his successor, Senator Murphy, in his period of office. He pursued a determinedly individual approach, and made no pretence of seeking to represent community standards. His actions in the area were, of course, only part of a much bigger canvas.

His assaults on the family have been so evident and so consistent that to disregard them is to bury one's head in the sand. He initiated legislative moves which could result in undermining marriage (the Family Law Bill), removing parental responsibility and authority (the Human Rights Bill), as well as promoting promiscuity through the availability of pornography. These moves were, of course, a quite deliberate expression of his personal philosophy in regard to marriage and family life, and they have been supported enthusiastically by humanists. It remains for those who have a higher view of marriage and the family to be equally determined that they shall not be so thoroughly destroyed.

Pornographic books of high quality have always managed to find their way into this country — unless there were powerful reasons why they should be excluded. What new evidence is there that they should now be allowed to come in with less restraint? It was Mr. Chipp who admitted "The Little Red School Book" and said this move would cause no harm. It was the same Minister who released materials to the sex shops but then had to restrict them. That is not the voice of prevailing community standards.

It is important to note that the concept of restricting books for adult sale cannot be compared with restriction of drugs or films. Whereas the drug or the commercial film is a once-only experience, and hence is essentially expendable, the book, once read, can be passed on to influence others. A drug is used, the theatre is visited; but a book is available for wide distribution. This makes restriction at the point of sale no more than a gesture of control. If such material is to be allowed in, the only possibility for truly responsible distribution appears to be to confine such books to libraries.

YOUTH MUST BE PROTECTED

The purpose of current legislative proposals is to enable pornography to be made available on a restricted basis. Since it is clear from The American Commission Report on Obscenity and Pornography that pornography quickly finds its way into the hands of minors, even when sale is restricted to "adult bookstores" (see Appendix 1), we may expect the 'R' book to follow the same pattern.

A restricted book has the same "forbidden-fruit" attraction to a teenager that a drug has. "Pushers" will quickly find it worth their while to peddle such books around the high schools. The payment is unlikely to be financial, however, since this provides an admirable opportunity for sexual seduction of the young. A change in the law in this area, therefore, will effectively remove all protection from the young. The argument, "let those who want it, have it", is a shallow and selfish one. It takes no account of what happens after the purchaser has finished with a book or magazine. Complaints are increasing that young people engaged on paper-drives for community-service purposes are often confronted with pornographic materials. This situation deserves attention as rigorous as that which seeks to prevent discarded drugs falling into the wrong hands.

Those who actually want to buy are very few, and the nature of pornography is such that the determined buyer obviously has a sexual problem. To feed fuel to this appetite is to invite wider problems. These will not readily be measurable, but the tip of the iceberg is already apparent. K.E. Davis and G.N. Braucht give some idea of where to look for adverse consequences when they say, "Exposure to pornography is part of a strongly deviant life style, including in some cases strongly homosexual patterns, and including in other cases a high level of heterosexual experience, with little regard for the quality and duration of the relationship".[9]

WHO SHOULD BE RESPONSIBLE?

Contemporary community standards are undoubtedly changing. While this may serve as a good reason for keeping criteria for censorship under constant review, **it does not justify using those same changing standards as the yardstick.** Rather, there is a case for requiring that a responsible, but disinterested, group of experts be entrusted with the responsibility to evaluate what is going to be in the interest of the community. This might involve relaxation of censorship in some areas, or being more restrictive at times. The heterogeneity of the country makes the use of prevailing community standards *per se* quite inappropriate. The influence which money has on the situation makes decisions the more difficult.

It is also a great hazard to have this responsibility vested in one whose position is determined by public vote. In such a sensitive area as censorship, no politician will calmly initiate a program of control which he believes necessary, but unpopular. He will not usually take steps which jeopardize his future career or seriously embarrass his own government. He is therefore forced either into a psychopathic role of proceeding regardless of the consequences, or seeking some compromise course which keeps him in office, yet does something to grapple with decisions that must be made. Where the outcome of decisions is unlikely to be clear for some years ahead, it is particularly tempting to legislate for popular opinion now, and leave a later government or Minister to deal with the consequences. A legislative program of rigid censorship will please one sector in the community while antagonizing others; a liberal approach simply reverses this. Our society is such that freedom from restraint now is generally preferred to assessing possible later consequences; hence, logically, political capital is derived from a liberalizing attitude to censorship.

Nor should the critical decisions in this area be in the hands of those with vested interests. Politicians and publishers have too much at stake to make unbiased judgements of the evidence. Similarly, the community as a whole is ill-equipped, and quite unable to respond sensitively to all the issues involved. The community should expect public servants, specially appointed to this responsibility, to respond more dispassionately to the available evidence. Most decisions could probably be made through the responsible judgements of a duly authorized board. Where doubt arises, it has been customary to seek a legal decision, and this democratic procedure should still be invoked. The implications of retaining such procedures have been critically evaluated by Cline[10], who proposes both a procedure and the kinds of criteria which might be used.

7

Pornography — Its Nature and Effects

Pornography is the attempt to insult sex, to do dirt on it.
D.H. Lawrence

THE NATURE OF PORNOGRAPHY

A definition may serve as a starting-point to distinguish pornography from other material often brought into consideration with it. The Kronhausens said that "pornography is characterized by an absence of the reality constraints that mark erotically realistic works of fiction. . . One might say that the primary aim is to create a state of increasing sexual arousal in the reader by portraying sexual relations in which all standards are violated and in which the only psychological feelings involved are lust and a mindless sexual joy".[1]

It should be apparent that this definition excludes many things on our bookstalls which often cause offence. Much literature, which can better be described as erotica, is produced to provide titillation and sexual arousal in the normal male. And its presence in the community may be sufficient to cause offence, especially to women. But it is important to recognize that pornography, especially hard-core pornography, is in a different category when its nature is considered.

EROTICA AND PORNOGRAPHY

Erotica typically arouses the male sexually to have erotic thoughts and intentions; and, to a lesser extent, women have also been shown to have a positive response to such material.[2] Pornography with subjects defined as normal can be distinguished from erotica in terms of the reactions which people report. D.Amoroso *et al*[3] report that undergraduate males gave a meaning to pornography different from that given to erotica. Typically, it was found that material rated as sexually-stimulating might be either "pleasant" or "unpleasant". Material identified as *arousing but unpleasant* may be labelled as pornographic, while erotica is that which is reported to be *arousing and pleasant.*

While making this broad distinction, it will become apparent that one is dealing with a *continuum* of which I have described the opposite poles, but in which there is a middle "grey" area where disagreement over definition will rage. Dispute over what should be done about pornography often arises because one group is defending availability of sexually-explicit material (for example, nudity), while the other side is referring to hard-core representations of bestiality and the like.

The above distinction found with normal male student populations cannot be maintained when material is presented to more deviant populations. It is clear from the vast pornography industry that there are many males who seek after pornography in an addictive fashion, apparently not experiencing either the revulsion of many normal subjects, or the satiation ("boredom") reported when normals experience forced-feeding.[4] Some evidence for this comes from H. Nawy's study[5] of patrons of pornographic films who demonstrate a high rate of attendance as well as a high level of promiscuous behaviour.

PORNOGRAPHY IS HATE

To understand why there could be different reactions, it is necessary to consider further what is the underlying meaning of pornography. This has been the subject of considerable psychiatric study in recent years by Khan and Winnicott, whose views have been brought to wider attention by Holbrook.[6] Central to his theme is the idea that the essential message of pornography is hate — which, of course, puts it far removed from the position where sex is seen to be the vehicle for the expression of love. This element of hate would explain why well-adjusted people instinctively react against pornography even when they may not understand why, whereas those with pent-up hostilities or frustrations may find something to which they can respond. Some of the elements are contained in the following:

> "... The champions of pornography make out that what they are trying to remedy are the inhibitions of our instincts through prudish traditions — they are trying to 'release' us. They are trying, they claim, to enable us to be more vital and feeling — to be 'ourselves' more, in the sexual realm. And yet, as Khan says, what pornography achieves is the opposite. In it, the images and words 'usurp' the natural functions of instinct. Instead of natural, loving feelings, moving towards 'meeting' another human being, we have an intense mental concoction of often brutal imagery — as in the cinema, where rape, and other gross acts of sadism are now frequent. The effect of these mental brutalities is to 'disregard the person and being of the characters'. We may observe this, even in 'girlie' magazines, in which the titillating way the girl is discussed, and her photographic exploitation as an object, destroy her personal unique qualities. This is the objection to the use of nudity in advertisements, too. It makes woman into a commodity thing. In all pornography, she is humiliated and subjected to contempt as a mere sex object. In her image, humanity

itself is degraded, by being deprived of value and subjected to hate, as the Jew or Negro is degraded in racist propaganda. Guilt and fear are not dispelled by pornography: on the contrary, it encourages us to enjoy hate in our attitudes to sex, and to have contempt for other people, especially women."[7]

The defence of pornography often follows the line that "a few dirty pictures won't hurt anyone", and "that sort of stuff has always been around for those who want it". Such a reaction is either naive or dishonest. The nature of pornography is such that its users are not content to stay with the "few dirty pictures" but must always move on to new material as the effect of familiarity blunts reaction. The similarity to a physical addiction is not a coincidence. There has been in recent years a pushing back of boundaries to permit more and more perverted material to circulate. It is still true in this country that even most supporters of pornography reject the free dissemination of pornography representing bestiality, incest, and assault on minors. Yet the bounds will be extended soon enough if we adopt a conciliatory attitude at a lesser level.

The defence of pornography, as being already available to those who seek it, rarely takes account of two further considerations:

(i) The hitherto-restricted availability has been a mark of disapproval of the society-at-large. Those who sought it out did so recognizing that they were at odds with the cultural norm. To permit free availability at this point is, in effect, to give endorsement to pornography by breaking the taboo associated with it. This is well-recognized by those who advocate the removal of restrictions. The implications of breaking taboos deserve serious thought, as it is very difficult to reverse decisions about social customs in this area.

(ii) For a small number of people to have illicit access to pornography is one thing; to permit free circulation of it is quite another. Even though point-of-sale restrictions may be placed on material so that minors do not buy it, it is clear that this protection disappears as soon as the material has been purchased (see Appendix 1). Thus the much-vaunted protection of children becomes no more than a hollow promise as soon as adults take their absolute freedom to see and read what they will.

As sexually-explicit material is widely defended today, it should be noted that a gradual "softening-up" approach was adopted in Denmark, so that people in that country failed to respond appropriately as explicit and pathological material was introduced step by step.[8] This deliberate policy prepared the way for the public acceptance of sex shows, including not only actual intercourse on stage, but group-sex and bestiality.[9] In this context, pornography was used deliberately to influence behaviour.

PORNOGRAPHY BRINGS PERVERSION

Pornography can also have its influence on behaviour in less-carefully-planned ways. The acceptance of perverse behaviour by many well-meaning people is matched by the acting-out of perversity by disturbed individuals who become a social hazard. We have had reports of the 37 boys murdered by a homosexual sadist, and the more recent Boston white woman forced to douse herself with petrol and destroy herself in a style presented on film in that city shortly before. There is a real risk that screening of "porno-violence" will have similar harmful consequences to those which followed the screening of "A Clockwork Orange" and "Dirty Harry".[10]

Such instances underline the importance of recognizing the intrinsic hate and hostility expressed through pornography. R. Stoller[11] maintains that pornography does not simply represent perversions, but is itself perverted, leading as it does away from the meaningful-relationship aspects of sex. Moreover, in answer to those who assert that pornography deserves freedom from the law because it lies in the area of victimless crimes, he would maintain that this underlying hostility means there is always a victim involved. Actors and models are humiliated, viewers are insulted, buyers are exploited.

There are two further senses in which one may associate pornography and perversion. First, the use of pornography may be seen as a form of sexual deviation in itself, of a voyeuristic type.[11] It serves as a poor substitute for a healthy sexual encounter based on commitment, so that, far from glorifying sex, it tends to destroy its meaning. Secondly, pornography is not an affirmation, but a denial, of life; and commercial pornography is a denial of life for the sake of money.[12] The similarly anti-sexual nature of much erotica has often been noted in the past [13,14]; but in pornography it goes further. Whereas in erotica the emphasis is removed from person to technique, from relationship to experience, in pornography a further detachment from reality occurs. Under the guise of unrestrained intimacy of a liberating kind, there is, in fact, a denial of any true intimacy and a great emphasis on domination — this latter becoming most evident with the sadistic pornography of flagellation. A whole range of analyses of the nature of pornography has been drawn together in the edited volume, "The Case against Pornography"[15], as well as in the individual members' contributions to "The Longford Report".[16]

THE EFFECTS OF PORNOGRAPHY

It is highly artificial to consider the effects of pornography in isolation from its nature; hence some indications have already appeared above of what pornography will do. Nevertheless, several further issues need to be raised which bear specifically on the question of effects.

At the simplest level, we may look for effects which are good or bad. It is necessary to go further and specify effects on whom, when, and under what conditions. A thorough evaluation would specify effects on individuals as well as on society-at-large. With individuals we should look for

(i) direct (causal) and indirect effects,
(ii) short and long-term effects,
(iii) hyperarousal or blunting.

In society-at-large we would seek for evidence of

(i) changes in directly-related social pathology statistics (such as sex offences),
(ii) changes in indirectly-related social pathology statistics (other crimes against persons or property),
(iii) changes in the incidence of sex-transmitted diseases,
(iv) changes in social attitudes to pornography (including revulsion or unaroused acceptance).

I have discussed evidence relating to some of these indicators elsewhere[17]. There is accumulating evidence for significant harmful effects, even though the numerous studies in this area are rather equivocal and liable to differing interpretations. The suggestion that there might also be some good effects is so commonly made that this will be given special consideration below.

PORNOGRAPHY AND ITS EFFECTS

It is important to realize that widespread confusion over the effects of pornography exists for several reasons. Until only a few years ago, the harmfulness was self-evident on moral grounds, but scientifically unproven. More recently, with the pressure to reject moral norms, the onus of proof has moved to experimental studies, the American Report of 1970 being one of the more important. The quality of that evidence was, however, severely flawed by the expectations of some of those contributing to the research. That the Commission Chairman was a prominent "civil liberties" man, who was also prepared to allow suppression of evidence which conflicted with the general findings, reflects badly on the defence of freedom of speech and information. And many have been persuaded to reject some of the most compelling evidence in the technical reports to the Commission on the grounds that it was contained in the dissenting minority-report of Hill and Link.[18] It must therefore be recognized that the evidence which these two writers brought to the attention of the general public, with the aid of a Supreme Court action, was equally based on the technical reports within the main body of data. That the majority report deserved criticism has been noted by Eysenck who says "the strictures on the authors of the majority report are unfortunately only too well taken".[19]

The evidence on effects is also difficult to evaluate because of the technical problems in studying them. The area has only recently become a subject for study. Methods are not yet refined, and many of the critical experiments which one might wish to do in theory are impossible in practice. Much of what has been done is largely irrelevant because of the restricted samples studied. It is no more suitable to draw conclusions about the effects of pornography on a sexually-disturbed man by using students under controlled laboratory conditions, than it is to assess the effect of a glass of spirits on an alcoholic by giving a test-dose to a university student. Many other methodological and statistical problems still cloud the picture.[20]

The evidence from studies of individuals and groups, which supports the view that pornography has harmful effects, may be summarized as follows:

(i) Comparison of sex-deviate groups and others using self-reports indicated a high desire among deviates (when compared with normals) to imitate what they see in erotic material.[21]

(ii) While many studies with normal subjects fail to demonstrate harm, there is evidence that a minority even within normal groups do experience an adverse reaction.[22]

(iii) That not only attitudes, but also actual behaviour, may be affected is shown by Walker, whose study of the aggressive sexual offender concluded that "the experimental group reported more frequently than the control group that pornography had led them to commit a sexual crime . . . had something to do with their being in hospital or prison . . . that their sexual behaviour had been affected by viewing erotic materials".[23]

(iv) The view that sex-crimes go down following the legalization of pornography must now be rejected as scientific nonsense. The widely-quoted Danish figures have been shown to be utterly misleading (see Chapter 5), and can be used in evidence only by those who refuse to examine the more recent data. I have reported elsewhere on the striking rise in rape statistics that has occurred since 1969 in Denmark, Britain, America, and now also Australia.[24] In New Zealand, the reported-rape rate remained practically unchanged at between 4 and 5 per 100,000 from 1962-1969, but since then a sharp rise has begun, reaching 8.6 by 1973.

The rise from 1970 to 1971 for Australia from 416 cases to 578 (39%) represents a significant upward variation from an already-rising trend. The drop in 1972 to 544 cases (representing a 6% decline from the previous year) proved insufficient to conclude that any significant decline might be beginning. The great danger in leaping to conclusions about data for any single year was shown when the 1973 figures became available. The upward trend was again apparent with a figure for the year of 680.There is every reason to remain deeply concerned at the trend of the last ten years — particularly when we recall that such reports represent only a small part of the total problem. That these trends are occurring in different countries which are concurrently disseminating pornography reduces the alternative explanations for the observed harm, and strengthens the case against pornography as a significant, though not necessarily causal, influence.

EVIDENCE FROM OTHER COUNTRIES

In order to establish the point logically, it is proper to ask, "What about countries where pornography does **not** circulate freely?". If there is no relationship between the steep crime rise and pornography, then such countries could also be expected to show a similar rise. If there **is** a relationship, then these other countries could be expected to have a stable or declining crime level.

Such a prediction seems conveniently easy to test. In fact, it is complex; pornography is only one influence among many: social structures differ widely: and statistics are not readily comparable across countries.

Some light on the question comes from a conference of directors of criminological research institutes held in Strasbourg in 1972. There, Selosse[25] reported on violent crime in several European countries. He has provided the rate per 100,000 inhabitants for various crimes against the person. The relevant figures for the present purpose are summarized in Table 1.

		1960	1965	1966	1967	1968	1969	1970
Sexual Assault	Austria		34.00	33.07	33.26	34.70		
	Sweden	6.80	7.60			7.60	8.40	
	Italy		14.32	14.36	15.13			
Rape, Attempted Rape & Indecent Assault	France		15.77			15.75		12.81
Wounding	Austria		43.66	43.98	48.54	46.62		
	France		81.16			92.38		84.02
	Italy	347.01	440.30	436.48	432.80			
	Sweden	116.10	151.10			212.50	205.30	

Table 1. Comparison of selected offences as reported to police in European countries. (Adapted from Selosse.)

More complete and recent data for England and Wales have been kindly provided by O.R. Johnston of the University of Newcastle-on-Tyne. These show, in summary, a rise for crimes of violence against the person from 17,950 in 1962 to 47,040 in 1971 (162% increase), and for wounding from 9,420 in 1960 to 22,010 in 1970 (133% increase). Population increase over the period was 4.6%.

A further important comparison may be made with figures from Singapore. This is a country which, according to a good many theoretical propositions, might be expected to have an escalating crime problem. It has one of the highest population-densities in the world; population has increased by one-third between 1960 and 1973, from 1,646,400 to 2,185,100. Urbanization is a feature of the development, as is the very high percentage of young people. Other sources of potential conflict and increased criminal activity include the multi-racial and mixed cultural character of the country. It is, moreover, an international cross-roads, and hence exposed to the risks of syndicated crime.

It is also a country where the Government has taken an unequivocal stand against "permissiveness", and where pornography is largely controlled. It therefore provides an interesting test of hypotheses for the development of crime in an urbanized contemporary society. Singapore is additionally suitable for investigation because it is a small country with well-recorded statistical data. It does not have the problem of integrating information from a number of independent police forces.

The figures on Table 2 give an indication of the trend for violent crimes generally, for all sexual crimes, and for reported rape and attempted-rape.

	1960	61	62	63	64	65	66	67	68	69	70	71	72	73
Total Violent Crimes	270	243	228	219	219	221	193	204	183	174	193	258	235	219
Total Sexual Crimes	9.05	8.58	7.60	8.24	6.95	7.53	6.98	8.35	6.76	6.66	7.57	9.00	9.87	9.61
Total Rape/ Attempted Rape	1.94	1.88	2.06	2.56	2.01	2.17	2.02	2.38	2.04	2.06	2.26	2.42	2.89	2.43

Table 2. Offences becoming known to the Singapore police. Figures based on official statistics and converted to the rate/100,000 population.

The rate of violent crime shows no signs of increasing when compared with a decade ago. Total sexual crimes show an increase over the last three years after a slight downward trend over the previous ten years. The extent of this is very slight at this point when level is taken into account. For rape and attempted-rape, the level remains fairly constant and very low.

This comparison gives some support for the view that a sharp rise in sexual assault is not an inevitable corollary of contemporary living. It provides a negative case to strengthen the argument from positive cases cited above. It is not conclusive. One important difference between Singapore, and the other countries discussed, is its predominantly-Asian population. The cultural norms undoubtedly influence the rate of crime and level of reporting. Nawy[26] notes that the Chinese in San Francisco are under-represented for sex crimes though over-represented numerically in the erotic marketplace of that city. Nevertheless, the important observation for Singapore is that offences of rape **are** reported, they are infrequent, and they show no signs of increasing in the way that such reports are increasing in countries which have permitted greater freedom to pornography. They were at a level comparable to Australia in 1960, and remain much the same today, whereas Australian figures have multiplied several times.

SUMMARIZING THE SITUATION

Since such data clearly take one a long way from the distribution of pornography, this is a convenient point to summarize some of the relationships which may be involved.

First, a country which accepts that sexually-explicit material, including pornography, is appropriate for public display and easy distribution, has made a value-judgement about the quality of human life. Pornography may have various influences on the way others are treated. It is an endorsement of exploitation and humiliation. In its more sadistic forms it condones and encourages psychological and physical hurt to others. It is therefore legitimate to look not only at the rate of sexual crimes *per se*, but at those broader expressions of hostility which are reflected in statistics of violent crime of other types.

Secondly, figures of the kind given above are crude measures, capable of interpretation in various ways. The relative stability of offences in Austria, Italy, and France (where "permissiveness" has not been encouraged by law) is an indication of a difference in trend from countries like Sweden, Denmark, or Britain. It is not, however, conclusive. The category "sexual assault" suffers from the disability of Danish data, in that all kinds of offences are lumped together, some increasing and some decreasing.

Thirdly, the relative levels for each country differ strikingly, and reflect cultural differences as well as reporting differences. What matters is not the actual level for any given country, but the appearance of **changes** from a base-level which may indicate that a new influence has appeared. In Sweden, for example, a great rise of offences against the person has occurred in recent years, but it still does not approach the higher level which has been relatively stable in Italy.

Fourthly, the trends from one country to another can be considered in relation to the time when pornography began to circulate freely. If this factor is a significant influence in the rate of sex crimes, then the time at which such changes occurred should show a close correspondence. In Britain and America, explicit materials have been available to the point where there has been public concern since the early 60s. In Denmark, the trend moved rapidly in the late 60s, with notable legislative changes in 1967 and 1969. In Australia, a notably conservative tradition changed quite abruptly in 1970, and has moved rapidly since. In New Zealand, the level of tolerance still focuses on magazines like "Playboy", and the advent of the sex shop is associated with 1974.

A study of trends in rape reports shows a persuasive correspondence with these dates, with a relatively stable picture being followed by an upward trend. In New Zealand, the upward trend has scarcely begun, while in the United States it has reached crisis level. The time-scales mentioned above correspond to figures given by Whitehorn.

> "In Britain, there were twice as many rapes known to the police last year as 10 years ago (893 as against 473) . . . (In Australia) there has been a big rise in the number of alleged rapes over the past few years — from 416 in 1970 to about 600 last year."[27]

Insofar as the "civil liberties" argument for free distribution of pornography rested on the Danish figures, the evidence has now gone so far the other way that its supporters should be among the leading exponents of a reversed policy. Indeed, in Britain this does now appear to be the case among responsible rationalists. At the recent announcement by the Home Secretary of measures to control pornography, a woman writer in the "Free-thinker" (May 17, 1973) said that these measures would be welcomed "by liberals, Liberationists, and all those who have some concern for the quality of life in our country today".

Finally, it is necessary to examine the other main argument of those who favour the free availability of pornography — which says that not only is it not harmful, but it may even be beneficial to some. This remarkable view derives its support from the catharsis theory of emotion, which asserts that those who have strong pent-up sexual tensions can achieve a vicarious experience through viewing sexual material, so that they become less likely to act out against others.

This theory achieved popularity when it was taken up from a study conducted by Feshbach,[28] not on pornography, but on aggression. The so-called "Feshbach hypothesis" proposed that the ventilation of aggression through fantasy would reduce the probability of enacting it against others.

It may be objected, of course, that it is a big leap from aggression to sex — although many will grant that the mechanisms governing expression and control are effectively comparable. The more significant objection, however, lies in the repeated failure of later workers to confirm the theory. On the contrary, the accumulated evidence now convincingly shows that the screening of aggression in films or on TV results in an **increase** of such behaviour in the viewer, both in the short- and long-term.[29] That the same trend could be predicted with pornography is readily apparent when one recognizes the hostile and destructive undertones which characterize pornography. (See Chapter 5).

DUBIOUS BENEFITS OF FRANKNESS

George Steiner is a literary critic who believes that the move to explicitness and pornography has had undesirable consequences. He criticizes the sadistic components of pornography because of their impact on contemporary society, and adds:

> "Today we live in an explosive, tired, overcrowded, edgy social situation. Everywhere there are fires simmering. Need one pour oil down them to make them even hotter?"[30]

When asked, "Can't you find a single benefit in the new frankness?", he replied:

> "This is the great loss in pornography, and I defy any social psychologist to show me that the release of fantasies in so public a way has caused one less case of mental anguish, one less case of frustration, or created one new masterpiece of fiction or drama or film."[30]

The other more recent line of argument was that, following availability of pornography in Denmark, there was a striking drop in offences like voyeurism and exhibitionism.[31] Taken in isolation, such evidence appears to indicate that the man who was previously a social nuisance has diverted his sexual energies to the more solitary pursuit of pornography.

It is now possible to dispel that myth by showing that in reality the pattern seen with violence is also apparent with pornography. The problems have become worse, not better. A police report from Denmark notes that sex offences are now more often serious than minor; and they have found that over the years since 1969 there has been an escalation of problems (for example, rape and attempted-rape figures rose from 27 in 1969 to 63 in 1972). Furthermore, just as there is increasing dismay that our society is coming to accept violence as normal, so, too, one effect of widespread pornography is that its values and meanings permeate society. If the message of pornography is one of hate and hostility, then its acceptance must have destructive consequences. Unfortunately, the truth of this is being reflected in the very statistics one might wish to consult for evidence. The indications from Denmark are becoming increasingly confusing as it becomes impossible to assume uniformity of data from year to year. Not only have the laws repeatedly changed so that overall figures become meaningless, but it appears that the tendency to report offences is going down quite markedly. When it is realized that pornographic materials are used in the schools for instruction, it is not difficult to understand that, after a few years, behaviour which young people would previously have reported as deviant, becomes acceptable as normal. This provides a possible explanation for the finding that some sex-crime trends have not gone up as dramatically as in other countries where the changes have been less extensive (for example, the 1972 figure for rape in Copenhagen was 51), and why the reports of offences against children have similarly declined from an earlier peak.

Such a trend is in no way reassuring. It indicates rather that, for reliable evidence in this area, it will be necessary to look to other countries where the confounding variables are fewer — though they, too, in due course could become similarly contaminated. It is to be expected that those who like to defend pornography will see these changes as supporting the view that no harm is demonstrable. It will, however, be a difficult position for them to maintain, in the face of the initial rises in those countries encouraging pornography, together with the absence of such rises in other places which have taken a conservative line (as outlined in Chapter 5).

Holbrook has drawn attention to this social-acceptance phenomenon, saying, "the toleration of perversion can have its own meaning, and can communicate abroad the implication that psychopathological 'solutions' are socially acceptable".[32] Richard Neville similarly notes that the effect of making pornography available is to destroy the family and encourage promiscuity.[33]

Perhaps the most helpful summary currently available would be the following:

> "It cannot any longer be argued with any degree of conviction that pornography, or the portrayal of violence, have no effect on the behaviour of the people who see these things on the screen, or read about them in books and magazines. . . Both behaviour and emotional reactions are affected, and the effects are not transitory. The evidence is admittedly indirect, but that is not really a valid point of criticism; much scientific evidence in the 'hard' sciences is of this kind, and is readily accepted on much the same level as direct evidence. . . What the argument is about is simply the nature of the society in which we wish to live, and in which we wish our children to live — neither more nor less."[34]

8

Can We Let Science Be Our Guide?

No wonder that a scientist — and no Christian either — has to say that "Science cannot exist without judgements of value".

C.A. Coulson in 'Science and Christian Belief'

Confidence in the findings of science has been a feature of the twentieth century. The scientific method is often represented as the only way of obtaining **real** knowledge. This confidence has not been as great in the life sciences as in biological or physical sciences, since the data are less-easily subject to experimental control. But more sophisticated statistics have overcome many problems of method and design so that a greater range of statements can be made. Nevertheless, it is still not appropriate to seek from experiments the answers to man's moral or ethical "decisions". Behind the findings of science lie important assumptions. The choice of experiments represents a value-judgement by the scientist. And the interpretation of the results rests on the balancing of the evidence; this can allow conclusions to differ widely from one to another.

It is dishonest to represent scientific studies as providing final answers to ethical dilemmas. No study ever finally **proves** anything — it simply contributes further information to an accumulating store of knowledge. If scientific data are to have value, they must be set within some value-system. For example, a finding from an experiment that confronting a child with the depiction of violence will, under certain circumstances, make him act more violently (Bandura 1969)[1], is a scientific result. The implications which can be drawn will vary. Some will see this as a good thing, the child being able more freely to ventilate aggressive tendencies which will only cause problems if they remain unexpressed. Others will say that an important part of emotional development is the establishment of self-control, and that, moreover, the acting-out of aggression could be dangerous to others. On the basis of this latter interpretation, one would advocate caution over allowing children access to violence (under the conditions of the experiment at least), whereas, with the first interpretation, the opposite recommendation would follow.

FUSING ETHICS AND SCIENCE

Who is right? The answer is not simply a matter of science. It involves a question of values, a consideration of priorities. Not all are prepared to spell out the basis for the recommendations they make, partly because the acceptance of science as a god-like agency in its own right has come to receive some support. But Jeeves argues:

> "Since ethical principles are **not** logically derivable from scientific findings, any attempt to elevate science to the level of an ethical system, which must be believed or accepted, immediately opens itself to abuse in that it means that particular scientists claim to derive **their** ethical beliefs from **their** science and then set these forward as the ones that **must** be accepted by all people".
>
> *[emphasis mine]* [2]

For the non-scientist it is worth identifying some of the difficulties involved in using scientific evidence in issues of social importance. It is difficult to challenge scientific studies without an awareness of the fragility of many of the findings, and the ways in which sweeping generalizations can often be drawn from limited results. The following points will be based mainly on the interpretation of psychological results, but the problems exist more widely:

1. "The main effect is the most important"

It is usual to suppose that the largest differences found as a result of an experiment are the ones which should receive most attention. For example, if 100 people were deprived of food for three days, and their behaviour at the next meal was compared with a group who had eaten normally, we should expect a massive difference in food consumption between the two groups. Even if 10% of the starved ate very little, attention would be paid to the eating of the majority as the major experimental effect.

Yet, we really learn very little from the big group who confirm one's expectations. Of far more interest is the group who do **not** behave as expected. What makes them different? Although numerically few, the really-exciting finds are more likely to be located in the exceptional result, rather than in the large group who behave as predicted. Conventional statistics have commonly resulted in such information being overlooked or lost. In recent years, findings on the effects of drugs have been made because of this attention to the abnormal few. It is attention to small and unusual effects which alerted people to the dangers of thalidomide and DDT. Such examples from medicine and ecology are now being multiplied.

The same principle is important for psychology. No less a person than Sir Michael Swann, Chairman of the B.B.C., has spoken of this, and courageously accepted a degree of responsibility:

> "If pharmaceutical drugs should be carefully controlled because they can on occasions lead to deformities, by what logic can films and television be exempt if they, too, produce undesirable effects,

> even if only in a few cases? All drugs now have to pass the most stringent tests to show they do not harm even the tiniest proportion of takers. Is violence on the screen totally different? Is it not up to us (the B.B.C.) to show that what we screen does **not** have ill effects, rather than up to others to prove that it does?"[3]

If 10,000 children watch violent films on TV, what matters more — that 90% show no measurable change, or that 10% show a change in attitude and behaviour? If 90% of adults viewing pornography were to show no adverse effects, should this cause one to disregard the 10% who show some evidence of harm (however defined)?

A tragic illustration of this problem has been presented by the case of Arthur Bremer, who shot Governor Wallace after being influenced by "A Clockwork Orange". Many think of these dramatic cases as so isolated that policies should not be influenced by them. Yet, a responsible journal carried this comment:

> "The frightening thing about quiet people like Bremer and Sirhan and Oswald is that there must be millions of them in the United States, holding their rage inside them, until — lacking the safety valve most individuals have — they explode. . . Even more frightening is the fact that we have known about them for years. A 1930 White House Conference on Youth estimated that there were 2.5 million children with well-marked behavioural difficulties, and since then things have become worse. There are now thought to be about 4 million such children under the age of 18, of whom 1.4 million are in acute need of psychiatric care, with only 473,000 receiving even minimal attention."[4]

It is unhappily true that politicians are more influenced by the 90% than the 10%, yet the real risk to a society arises from the disturbed minority within it. It is apparent, from the shockingly-high figures for crimes of all sorts, that disturbance of many kinds runs at a higher level than it did. The sharp increases seen in recent years in offences like shop-lifting and vandalism, or the escalation of teenage suicides, illegitimate births, and venereal disease, provide some kind of social thermometer of change, which by any standards must surely give cause for concern.

The fact is, that small but significant effects are being overlooked, although they may contain the key information we need for decisions on social legislation. The harmful effects of pornography, and adverse reaction to violence in the media, are good examples of this. **All** need to accept restrictions for the sake of those who are at risk. Recurrent experiences of sky-jacking and terrorism, as well as wild-cat strikes, have provided painful evidence of the way in which the activities of an unscrupulous few can hold a whole community to ransom. We accept control of drugs and licensing of guns, not because the **majority** would otherwise become junkies or killers, but because of the disturbed minority who can produce personal and social chaos. The same principle can equally apply in the area of psychological harm.

2. Definition of harm

Under the previous heading, harm was mentioned but not defined. Psychological experiments may demonstrate "effects", but whether these are harmful, neutral, or beneficial cannot always be decided on scientific grounds. Physical harm is more readily agreed about because of its influence on physical survival, but the "harm" identified in studies in the area of sex and violence must be defined in terms of some value-system. It may be helpful to distinguish pyschological from moral or religious harm, the former being more readily subject to scientific definition. A discussion of this differentiation has been offered elsewhere.[5] But there are some concepts which obviously involve both psychological and moral constants.

An important example is that of sexual arousal. Erotic books and films explicitly aim to produce sexual arousal, and with modern techniques are highly effective in normal individuals. Pornography has a similar intention, which appears to be realized with the sexually-disturbed, but which often produces an opposite effect in sexually-well-adjusted individuals. That such effects occur is not seriously disputed, but it is a matter of disagreement whether arousal produced in this way is harmful or not. "What is wrong with stimulating a natural appetite?" is a common reaction. Indeed, some would go further and argue that the use of erotica may be beneficial to sexually-inhibited individuals, and should therefore be made more widely available.

There need be no disagreement about the acceptability of sexual arousal *per se,* or of helping those with a problem in this area.

This is not to say that scientific evidence is inadmissible altogether. The problem lies in defining what constitutes harm for the individual. It is possible to evaluate attitudes to sexuality, to other people, and to erotica, and measure whether certain changes occur. In practice, this is methodologically difficult; and there still remains the problem that what some call harm, others will see as beneficial. At a broader level it may be possible to agree when harm of a psychological kind occurs. Studies which have tried to measure harm have looked sometimes at individual response, while others have looked at inter-personal behaviour. Measures like reports of rape are crude and open to many questions, but at least there is little disagreement that here is an undesirable piece of behaviour. Intrusions by one person on the privacy of another, and the incidence of sex-transmitted diseases, can also be generally agreed to represent suitable measures. More subtle measures would obviously be desirable; but, failing these, gross measures can give some indication of what is happening. Chapter 7 deals with evidence of this kind.

As soon as moral values are introduced, a number of issues arise which can change the whole picture. The concept of lust is a moral one, not a scientific one. This moral concept would distinguish sexual arousal associated with a loved person from that stimulated in other ways. "Arousal" created by a spouse is different in quality from that produced in response to a picture, a film, a book, or another person.

The harmful effects of salacious material, suggestive advertising, and the like, are therefore best defined in moral terms of incitement to lust. Scientific measurements do not offer any evidence on this matter, and so cannot be said to bear on the question of moral harm in any useful way. We must conclude that the Christian will take a distinctive position about the significance of erotica; without in any way prejudicing the scientific evidence, he or she can come to a resolute condemnation of its inherent harm and to firm opposition to its indiscriminate availability.

It should be noted that the importance of the moral argument, which will be stressed by those willing to accept moral standards, has been related here to sexually-arousing material, or erotica. This covers much material widely available today, and extends far beyond the boundaries of pornography.

Similar assessments based on moral values will also lead the Christian to be more sensitive than others to the potential harm in other areas of human influence. Materialism in advertising (greed), and irresponsible attitudes to work (sloth) may serve as examples from the "seven deadly sins".

3. From the laboratory to life

For exact measurements, the scientist likes to carry out experiments where he can control the situation he studies. Laboratory work is therefore of great value in sorting out one influence from another more exactly than can be done in field studies. However, the very control itself, and the restrictions imposed by the laboratory, may make the results of no relevance. It is no surprise to the scientist to find conclusions coming from laboratory findings different from those found outside; but most others are inclined to see an experimental result as likely to be **more** valid than a field study. "The validity of applying experimental findings to new situations, new groups of persons, and new procedures, depends on the degree to which the original experiment was representative of the new situations. In general, the greater the difference between the original resource setting and any other subsequent application, the more cautious must be the extrapolation attempt."[6] Evidence presented to the American Commission on Obscenity and Pornography[7] was of both types. Evidence which could lead to very different conclusions was obtained among the studies, and it must be a matter of judgement which results are to be taken more seriously.

When the question of possible harm is involved, there is a strong ethical case for taking more note of those which indicate harm than those which fail to find it. In practice, for obscenity and pornography, it is generally the field studies which suggest harm. Particular examples of the kind of evidence often used are given in Chapter 7.

4. The cause and effect problem

Much of the scientist's time is spent in trying to test what actually causes certain things to happen. In practice, he most often has to settle for inferring a cause without having final proof of this.

Psychological studies are specially open to question in this respect. Many relationships which **appear** to be causal prove only to be associations.

An amusing example of the misleading possibilities which may arise is given by Eysenck:

> "To know that A and B are correlated does not tell us whether A has caused B, B has caused A, C has caused A and B, or whether an even-more-complex chain is involved. The point is brought out very clearly in the well-known story of a little German village where there was an almost perfect correlation between the presence of newborn babies in a house and storks on the roof. This correlation was not due to the storks being responsible for delivery of the babies; it was due rather to a superstition obtaining in this village that storks brought good luck when a baby was expected. They were even thought to help the prospective parents to have children. Consequently, any couple that wanted to have children would put up a stork nest on the roof so that the desire to have children was the causal factor in attracting the storks to a particular home."[8]

Since the real relationship between observations is very commonly uncertain, even for those actually carrying out studies, how very easy it is for others to be misled or confused. Over-simplification by the mass-media adds to this difficulty, as modest results are blown up into extravagant claims.

For example, Farmer (1972) made recommendation that masturbation among teenagers should be encouraged by parents, stating:

"Since it appears that guilt-free masturbation in childhood and adolescence **contributes** to later sexual responsiveness, the censorship on this topic in the home must be regarded as a serious problem."
[emphasis mine][9]

The word "contributes" seeks to indicate that masturbation was at least one of the causes for the association found with later sexual activity. Actually, the nature of the link cannot be shown to be **causal.** Both observations could easily stem from a common link, such as the type of home background, the attitude to sexuality by parents, or the level of sex-drive. Yet it is from this observation, together with the finding that some sexually-disturbed patients achieve some help from masturbation in adulthood, that he went on to say:

"I recommend that (i) parents should not censure childhood masturbation, except to point out the advantages of privacy, and (ii) parents should encourage children to masturbate regularly and experimentally after puberty".

Whatever view one may hold regarding masturbation as a piece of behaviour, it should be emphasized that recommendations based on pseudo-scientific evidence must be exposed as the product of conclusions drawn from personal opinion and limited observation. They are dangerous when cloaked in the scientific *mystique.*

Because two events commonly occur together, this is not evidence that one **causes** the other, even though one may always occur before the other. Yet sweeping recommendations are sometimes made on the basis of such loose relationships. Those who advocate **tighter** controls must, of course, also be wary of concluding that rising statistics of crime have a causal connection with more permissive laws or attitudes. The causal connection is one possibility. It is also possible that permissive attitudes and rising crime rates both arise from a more basic common cause. So, for example, it is fruitless to try to argue that a rise in the incidence of venereal disease has been **caused** by increased pornography in Scandinavia, even though the parallel rises might appear to suggest this. It would, however, be much more significant to show that both rises shared a common cause, such as a breakdown in family life-styles, or a rejection of Christian morals. It would be more significant because the identification of a root-cause like this means that changes at that level can produce benefits in **both** the problem areas. It is, of course, the Christian's belief that the root-causes of the evils in society are to be found in man himself, and that a fundamental change is a necessary preliminary before more widespread benefits can result.

5. Direct and indirect effects

It is easy to demonstrate the direct effect of sticking a pin in a balloon. The result is dramatic, obvious, and undisputed. A scientific experiment is not needed to prove a direct link between the pin and the burst balloon. Indirect effects are, by their very nature, more elusive and contentious, yet no less important. That pollution in the River Rhine should influence living conditions in Sweden is not readily apparent, but should not be ignored. That penguins in Antarctica show DDT traces, even though DDT has never been used there, indicates a complex chain of events of great significance. Mercury-poisoning from fish, cancer from smoking, and many other examples from the physical world are becoming pressingly important. Survival of the species depends on taking adequate precautions before such indirect but powerful chains overwhelm us.

No less must the same kind of relationship be recognized in the psychological and moral sphere. It appears that children in Sweden who were never required to study vigorously, but were allowed to do what they would when they wanted, now have difficulty in holding down jobs, because they lack persistence and do not have a solid body of knowledge on which to build. The child who has never learned limits of acceptable behaviour when young must continue to define his limits as he gets older, so that, with increased distress and danger to himself and others, he becomes the rebellious and violent teenage student.

An alarming but well-reasoned discussion of imitation of violence has been offered by L. Berkowitz and J. Macaulay.[10] They studied the rises in criminal violence which followed the assassination of President Kennedy in 1963, and the Speck and Whitman crimes of 1966. Sharp increases in crimes were such as to lead the authors to propose something like a contagious effect arising from the publicity given to those events. Any who wonder what is the effect of giving wide publicity to shocking crimes should study this evidence thoughtfully.

A long-term and complex chain of events is difficult to identify, and dispute will often arise as to what causes what. However, there is wisdom in caution where people could be harmed. It certainly appears that aspects of permissiveness have brought many social problems in their wake. Some aspects are more readily brought under control than others, and should be the focus for concentrated and rigorous action. The pornography industry and the exploitation of violence for entertainment are two obvious examples. With mounting evidence of **direct** harmful effects (and no evidence of benefits), we may be confident that the **indirect** effects are even more extensive and damaging. We cannot afford to wait for final proof of indirect effects, because this is, by the very nature of the case, impossible to obtain. We should respond rather to the accumulation of social statistics, which together make clear that there is already a great deal that needs correcting. Escalating figures relating to crime, disease, and disturbance simply emphasize that we delay only to our peril.

6. Cause and precipitant

The evidence surrounding us that people's lives are in disarray is overwhelming. High rates of divorce, abortion, adultery, and murder are but the more tangible statistics of social confusion. To say that such behaviour is "caused" by what people see on TV or read in books is, of course, too simple. Yet this does **not** mean that these influences can be treated as if they were without effect. The gibe that "no girl was ever seduced by a book" is a classic example of the simple-minded defence of material that deserves to be roundly condemned.

In addition to the complexity of cause and effect discussed above, the significance of events as **precipitants** must be noted. Thus, a violent film may not be the cause of a man's violent behaviour, yet it can precipitate an act that would otherwise not have occurred. A young man viewing an erotic film is not made lascivious instantaneously; but the film may stir passions which would otherwise remain dormant or under control. Most perceptive parents will observe their children acting out the behaviour of their heroes on TV. To say that a child was disturbed **before** he modelled an aggressive act on TV in no way removes the responsibility of adults for ensuring that the child's disturbance is not increased.

With adult material, it is a poor argument to say that the average adult can see sex or violence portrayed and come away unchanged. Even if this were true (which is unlikely), the real issue revolves around those who can not cope with an inflamed imagination. The problem for adults of only marginal adjustment — that is, those who are emotionally unstable and who only just manage to preserve a sufficient balance to continue in the community — is an **increasingly serious** one. As films become more powerfully realistic through technical advances, the boundary between fantasy and reality becomes blurred even for the normal viewer. A film becomes no longer a spectacle to be viewed, but a total experience to be entered into. The marginally-adjusted person has the greatest difficulty in preserving the boundaries between fantasy and reality. We break these down only at great danger to all.

9

Some Common Objections

Our calling is to be critical of our times. We may be called to protest, too. We should have protested and protested in love, not in hate and anarchy, because we care for freedom and humanity, and hate all sin and unrighteousness.
H.R. Rookmaaker

Anyone prepared to question a prevailing trend is soon enough called upon to defend his actions. Those who see no harm in the present decline in standards are the first to discourage those who speak out. Even those who dislike the decline will often find reasons to criticize the activist; some cannot see how a stand for high standards can be justified; others, although their conscience is pricked to participate, prefer not to "rock the boat".

Many of the objections revolve around the extent to which the State should involve itself in people's private behaviour. The importance of civil liberties is stressed by those who wish to see the State exercise less control, and the philosophy of John Stuart Mill is given prominence. Others stress the importance of distinguishing sin from crime, referring to the Wolfenden Report for support. Behind these issues is the difficulty of defining what standards should prove acceptable in contemporary society; this has the obvious conclusion that, if there are no agreed standards, then no clear principles can be established.

All these issues are sufficiently complex to deserve detailed attention by experts; and much has been written. Broadly, the writing is from one or the other of two positions. The "civil liberties" position, which stresses individual freedom of choice, denies the right of the State to intervene in personal morality, and rejects absolute standards of moral conduct, is popular today. Briefly this could be labelled as a *my right* position. The other position derives from Christian teaching and might be labelled a *my responsibility* position. It recognizes that the needs of others may take priority over one's own wishes. It questions whether personal behaviour can ever be divorced from its consequences for others. And, to be able to offer anything constructive at all, it involves a belief in revelation which provides universal rules for living.

Having distinguished these two positions, some of the common issues may now be considered briefly. A fuller discussion of these issues may be found in books by Barclay,[1] Triton[2], and Anderson.[3]

1. "What right have you to interfere in the affairs of others?"

This question is a central expression of those who proclaim a civil libertarian view-point. It illustrates well that we are moving towards both a permissive society and a *laissez-faire* society — in which one does not break rules because no-one makes any, and in which "you leave me alone, and I'll not interfere with you". At first sight this sounds like freedom for all; but, in fact, the result is licence for some at the expense of many.

The question as asked usually has an aggressive undertone, since a sense of personal threat is implied. However, the question may be legitimately rephrased, "What responsibility have I to be concerned for the welfare of others?" So expressed, it is clear that all in a democracy must exercise this relationship if the rights of all are to be protected. It does, of course, mean that one must have reason to believe that intervention in the affairs of others is for good reasons and soundly based. The ethic of Christian concern should provide such a basis.

Interestingly, one sees this approach used by others, too, when some of the less-personal issues of morality are at stake. For example, the reasons advanced for seeking to prevent French nuclear-testing in the Pacific Ocean have a very close parallel to those which may be advanced for seeking restraint of pornography. Consistency would demand concern and action in **both** areas. Both involve intervening in the plans of others on the ground that harm could occur, and the risk is sufficiently great to override the freedom of others to act unilaterally. Both relate to harm which would be delayed and hard to specify exactly, but one need not doubt the reality in either instance.

This responsibility for others is especially pressing where the needs of the young, the weak, and the disadvantaged are concerned; indeed, Biblical teaching concerning one's neighbour is even broader, and includes even one's enemies. Such a willingness to put the needs of others before one's own self-interest is a concept which is increasingly little-understood in our contemporary hedonistic society.

2. "The law has no place in the bedroom."

This *cliché* is widely quoted to imply that what a person chooses to do in private is his own affair, and should not be the subject of legal sanction. As a **general** proposition, it makes a worthwhile point; indeed, the law should intervene as little as possible in private lives. But it derives from the view that we can isolate private from public behaviour — an arbitrary distinction not fully sustained even by Mill.

The development of psychological knowledge has blurred the boundaries to the point that such a distinction is meaningless. What a man does in privacy affects his subsequent behaviour and relationships.

This argument is commonly used to justify pornographic materials in private homes but not in public, and to defend the removal of legal sanctions against homosexual practices. However, the principle is only viable up to a point. Other considerations arise to override the principle. The law recognizes this in its retention of sanctions against rape and incest. There are, in other words, restrictions on what can be done in private. To subscribe without restriction to the view that the law shall **never** intervene in the bedroom is to strike a blow for the legalization of rape and incest. Not many will seriously advocate this. Failing this absolute position, it is always proper to assess the relative importance of personal liberty and social responsibility.

3. "Censorship is anti-democratic."

This is a superficial assessment of the real value of censorship. A serious consideration of the implications of having no censorship soon makes clear that a generally-agreed scheme of quality control is far more compatible with democratic principles than the removal of such controls.

Traditionally, the law has accepted this responsibility for interpreting community standards even at the risk of infringing individual freedom. As long as the majority was prepared to accept that it was proper for the law to act in this protective way, censorship and similar constraints on freedom of action operated with little question. Today, however, personal freedom is often prized more highly than the good of society generally; so politicians and legislators are being forced into the position of extending the boundaries of personal freedom so widely that those least able to object suffer most. The law must surely recognize a human right to protection from offence that many anti-censorship enthusiasts have forgotten. In the words of Ruth Brine, "If some have the right to pornography, others have an equal right not to have it foisted on them".[4] Or, as Haynes has put it, "If individual freedom demands that person X can read document A, it also demands that person Y may avoid reading it if he so desires. Thus, there must always be restrictions on the **display** of material". *[emphasis mine]* [5]

Ironically, those libertarians, who publicly seek to convince us that there are no standards, and that there should therefore be no censorship, prove to be vacillating and inconsistent when pressed. Current censorship policy is to allow adults to see, read, and hear what they please (even in spite of 44% of the Government's party-support indicating disagreement[6]), and yet some violent material is restricted. Consistency would require both types of material to enjoy free circulation.

Similarly, when humanists are challenged with the idea of disseminating material that promotes bestiality, they react as if some standards are desirable after all. Bestiality **for the moment** goes beyond their relative standards in Australia, but there is no reason to suppose that this will last. Already a TV writer has promised such displays as entertainment in the home within two years. Subtle moves to gain acceptance for incest are already under way, and forward planning is going on for this to be featured in films.

The foolishness of depending on shifting contemporary standards, rather than unchanging principles, may be illustrated from a letter written in evident disgust to a London paper, and captioned, "What is obscene?":

> "Someone recently sent me a magazine, which has a large circulation and is often bought by teenagers, which contained an enthusiastic description of men excreting in women's faces with, of course, full glamorization and justification, together with other vivid descriptions of perversions.
>
> "I sent this to the Director of Public Prosecutions, for his opinion. He informs me that this is not obscene. It would seem that the word 'obscene' now is so meaningless that it might well be deleted from the vocabulary; but if it goes, so will, by implication, concepts such as decent and indecent, human and anti-human, lawful and lawless."[7]

When freedom becomes the freedom to hate, then joy becomes the joy of pain.

4. "Let a man go to hell in his own way if he wants to."

It is only in the area of obvious moral conduct that such a suggestion can be made. And such a policy of non-interference has only the superficialities of compassion. Taken logically, this would require us to allow a man to commit suicide without intervening. It also runs counter to an increasing amount of legislation which seeks to protect people from themselves. Compulsory forms of insurance and consumer-protection laws assume that people cannot always be relied on to act wisely even for self-interest. There are times when even adults need protecting from themselves; and to fail to act in such a situation is anti-compassionate.

An interesting example of the results of a "hands-off" policy was seen early in 1972 when Governor George Wallace was shot by Arthur Bremer. It was reported that Bremer wrote in his diary, "I saw 'A Clockwork Orange' and thought about getting Wallace during the film." When found guilty, and asked if he had anything to say, he responded, **"All I wish is that you had protected me from myself"**.

[emphasis mine][8]

Mature adults may be able to see such films and show no obvious adverse effects. But it is the emotionally-unbalanced or criminally-inclined whom we may properly fear for. Those intellectuals who insist on freedom for corrupt material to circulate often add, "Of course I would not want it for myself; I am only defending the rights of others who do". A fine principle indeed, but spoilt by the fact that the ones who do want it are so often disturbed. A Texas Grand Jury report said:

> "We believe most of those who seek out today's entertainment more than once must be morally sick or perverted."[9]

5. "There are more important issues."

The presence of pornography and salacious literature in a community may not be the world's greatest evil. It is easy to point to major issues like poverty, war, racism, and many more, as more pressing issues for attention. Commonly, those who so object are doing little enough in a self-sacrificial way in these other areas, so the criticism loses some of its edge. Nevertheless, there are others who do see such issues as more pressing, and who are involved. Especially is this true of the student generation, who demonstrate real involvement over issues like war and ecological destruction.

First, therefore, one may say that each person is responsible for combating evil where he can. To be concerned about declining standards of morality is not to ignore other major and obvious issues, but to be active where action can be effective. Barclay notes that "there is not a problem threatening this or any other country just now which is not a moral problem".[10]

Secondly, it may be that the real driving-force of moral involvement in issues like war and poverty will be progressively dissipated as we permit the media to saturate us with hedonism, violence, and trivial materialism. While speaking at an international congress in Bonn, Mary Whitehouse said:

> "Whatever may be the motivation behind the present flooding of Western society by porn, the fact remains that sex, which is God-given and which is the fount of man's greatest creativity, is becoming in-turned and therefore destructive. Addiction to porn involves people in themselves. It can so pre-occupy them as to change their attitudes to life. As their obsession grows, so they become less and less concerned with the great political and social questions of their day, and consequently more and more ripe for dictatorship."[11]

Thirdly, we must not underestimate other powerful, eroding influences of salacious and pornographic material. The resulting shift in perspective of what values are worth preserving, the ready cultivation of an attitude of exploitation of others, and the acceptance of lust as the norm, will all dilute any impulse to involve oneself in the wider needs of others.

Fourthly, we must face the reality that these changes do not remain simply at the level of personal attitudes and values. Inevitably they spread to infect the relationships occurring within families and society. Responding to assertions by Mgr. Walsh that uncontrolled pornography leads towards loose living, the increasing practice of trial marriages, and far-reaching breakdown in community standards, the Victorian Chief Secretary, Mr. Rossiter, said:

> "The family as a unit must be preserved, and those forces in the community which are seeking to disrupt and destroy it must be stopped. The Third World forces have their eyes on a gigantic take-over of the Western world; and, without a doubt, pornographic, subversive, and pseudo-permissive practices are part of their arsenal for the capture of the Western mind. A breakdown of standards under the present Federal Labor Government can mean only one result . . . — a takeover by forces alien to our system of living."[12]

These examples should be sufficient to caution the reader against an unthinking fanaticism for either repression or unwarranted intervention in the affairs of others. Men of good will are seeking a balanced position where good can prevail and evil can be rejected. We are in danger of moving too far away from effective control of those unhealthy and calculatedly-destructive influences which are at work in society, and which, if left to develop, will produce a very different pattern of life. Those who are optimistic enough to believe that the developments are worth promoting experimentally are irresponsibly refusing to take account of the evil in men's hearts, which will triumph if not countered with continuing vigilance.

The removal of restrictions against exploitation of many kinds has now gone too far. Unless we respond soberly at this point and press for a healthy corrective, we shall either be forced into an extremist reaction or "backlash" of a most undesirable type, or be projected into the disastrous anarchy desired by our new totalitarians.

6. "We've always had this kind of problem — what's new?"

It is true, there has been no overnight change either in values or in what is being portrayed. Yet the gradual changes **have accelerated,** and some new facets need recognition. The demand for "realism" in films may be traced back to the influence of the positivist philosophers. In a detailed study of trends in art as they relate to culture, Rookmaaker argues that the move towards presenting realism in the nineteenth century emphasized only one facet of life. He writes that "true humanity, being much more than factuality, was left out of account".[13] We see the sequel to that today. The explicit depiction of some aspects of life without any sense of balance, and in isolation from other aspects, inevitably means that all that emerges is a distorted and misleading travesty. Rookmaaker continues:

"Realism, or rather, naturalism, in books and films today, for example, including all the facts of sexuality, has been prepared for, and was propelled on by, the nineteenth-century type of art we have been discussing. Since the eighteenth century there has been a constant reduction of the 'old' moral principles, a *demasque* leaving us at the end amidst the ruins of the one-time Christian consensus."[13]

Yet, to say that a trend has been present for a long time is no reason to disregard it (ask any ecologist!). Nor must we suppose that the level of impact remains unchanged. We must ask what the eventual outcome could be if the change continues.

It is necessary here only to summarize points that have now become clearly identifiable, so that we no longer accept prevailing trends with equanimity.

(i) The rapid advance in printing techniques in recent years now means that material can be disseminated widely and cheaply to a literate audience. This has made it a great deal easier for small subversive elements to infiltrate their ideas; where previously they could have been contained safely within a free society, they now become more of a threat to all.

(ii) Great advances in colour-printing make pornography no longer a dirty, cheap production. Pornography can be produced at a level of quality which will more readily seduce people into accepting it as legitimate. It becomes harder to reject such material on the grounds that it "lacks artistic merit".

(iii) More generally, the ease of communication and movement which we enjoy in our "global village" means that standards in one country influence standards around the world. The Danish experience well illustrates how a policy adopted in one place has major repercussions around the world. No community can easily maintain high standards when others around us adopt lower ones. The philosophy in films is very obviously being promoted internationally through theatres and television. A parochial attitude must be replaced by a global concern.

(iv) Pornography has always been around, but only under sufferance and through disreputable sources. Today, the evidence of the American Commission on Pornography and Obscenity, as well as the Longford Committee Report in Britain, reveals a multi-million-dollar industry. The argument that "the few who need it should have it if they want it" is shown up to be utterly specious. Either the "few who need it" prove to be many more than anyone ever suggested; or if they really are so few, they have an unbelievably voracious appetite for buying pornography in a compulsive fashion; or else the wide availability has drawn in many millions of people to accept what was previously rejected. One single explanation makes a mockery of the civil libertarian defence of pornography; that all three explanations may well be operating makes the whole matter one of urgency.

10

Is There A Basis For Standards?

> *A change in the degree to which the law of God is enforced in society does not in any way alter our ideal. The humanists are wrong to say that morals must change with changing circumstances.*
> *A.N. Triton*

The answer to this question is not self-evident; and, in view of all that has preceded this question, it will be clear that each person can only present a viewpoint based on certain assumptions.

The humanist's assumptions lead him to the point where what is personally satisfying is also acceptable. Together with the person who has adopted a situation-ethics philosophy, he will say that there are no absolute standards of right and wrong. Such a philosophy makes it difficult, if not impossible, to provide a legal framework for issues of morality. In addition, one must take account of those in the community who believe there is no real justification for laws at all, as well as those who seek the overthrow of law.

Traditionally, it has been Christian morality which has had the most powerful influence on our laws. So it is proper to ask whether this *can* still provide a basis for standards today; and, if it can, *should* it do so? Those with a Christian conviction have no doubt that there are standards to be derived from the Bible. Even though these often suffer from a variety of interpretations, the notion that some things are good while others are harmful is generally believed by enough Christians to form the basis for decision-making. What one does about the bad (ignore it, ban it, combat it,) will still be a basis for debate; but the general principle is a big step away from those who will not accept that anything is wrong in itself.

It is essential to consider the possible outcome of discarding the traditional Christian teaching that some things are right and some wrong. The alternative of saying that everything will be judged by prevailing community standards, regardless of moral absolutes, needs to be explored to its logical conclusion. One outcome is that behaviour like homosexuality and adultery can readily be accepted as normal. There will be no basis for rejecting any sort of sexual deviation as abnormal, or sick, or immoral; traditional protection of women, children, and the weak will be disregarded. The seduction of children will be followed by acceptance of incest, bestiality, porno-violence, and ritual murder. This sequence is based on the evidence of non-Christian countries, past and present.

RELIGION STILL COUNTS

Any who say that those who accept a morality based on religious belief are nowadays in a minority, must come to terms with Hans Mol's results of a recent survey of religion in Australia. He states:

> "Our findings suggest that in Australia those who are involved in their religion have different moral expectations from those who are not. Religion still makes a difference. It is certainly too soon to announce the demise of religion in this field. An English study [1] found that the majority of its respondents, especially the young, wanted the churches to express their opinions on moral and social matters. In this study there were also ten times as many people who wanted religion to have more influence, as people who wanted it to have less. All this suggests that the days of self-chosen morals certainly have not arrived, and that in Australia, as in Britain, a majority of the people are still seeking moral guidance from somewhere." [2]

Mr. Chipp, in his policy speech of 1970, referred favourably to a book, entitled "Obscenity and Public Morality", which gives some guidance in the area of obscenity:

> "It suggests that the essence of obscenity lies in making public that which is private, in trading on intimate physical processes and acts, or on physical-emotional states, thereby degrading the human dimension of life to a sub-human or merely physical level. The book goes further; it says that television scenes of the suffering of wounded soldiers, or televised interviews which seek to exploit the reactions of victims of emotional crises for public titillation, are obscenities as gross as any sexual display."

Even using this single principle, there is much currently being released under the 'R' certificate which must qualify for the label of obscenity. "The Devils" is promoted as the depiction of "hideous events, explicit and highly graphic". Similarly with "Straw Dogs", of which actress Susan George is reported as saying, "They've had me stripped and raped in every film I've been in recently. But 'Straw Dogs' was the very end. No more: there's a limit and I've reached it!" One may surely question whether the 'R' certificate is being used as an opportunity for films of quality or simply as an excuse for every kind of obscenity.

Even while the debate continues regarding where contemporary standards lie, it still remains that the formal criteria are unchanged. The Federal laws regarding films and books still outlaw material described as "blasphemous, indecent, or obscene". It is difficult to see how these words can be so mutilated to allow much which is currently being released.

A summary of some of the existing laws is provided in Appendix 2 for the reader who wishes to see the law enforced.

A CHALLENGE FOR CHRISTIANS

With this increasing diet of sex and violence, which trades on intimate physical processes, the theatre-goer is in danger of becoming a professional Peeping Tom. The freedom to choose wholesome entertainment is fast going, as even television takes to screening 'R'-type material. The words of the former Governor-General of Australia, Sir Paul Hasluck, are more true today than when he first spoke them in 1971:

"At present, in Australia, I would suggest that there is more constant and persistent invasion of privacy by evil influence than by good. What is lewd and suggestive is persistently thrust under notice. What is violent and criminal is presented romantically, and successful greed and very high earthly emoluments of sin are shown with glamour in ways that make it difficult for even the youngest and most carefully-protected to avoid contamination. The stimulation of sexuality and aggression is constant. One of the consequences of the new attitudes is that the right or the power of society to take action to protect any of its members, even the innocent, from these influences, or to check the attacks on their privacy, is being challenged.

"I wonder whether the Churches are doing all that they might do. Let me confess that sometimes I have found difficulty, when hearing some pronouncements, in understanding why persons who profess to give religious leadership dwell in such a shadowy land trying to distinguish between what is good and evil, between what is clean and what is dirty, what is true and what is false, what is one's duty towards a neighbour and what may cause a brother to stumble.

"If our society ceases to be one in which the view of man as a spiritual being prevails over the view of man as an animal, capable only of animal antics and animal relationships, the impending changes in the rules of society and the standards of conduct will, I am sure, bring confusion, distress, danger, and eventually collapse. Religious people have to join the struggle, and do it, not simply by giving shrill cries of alarm at every instance of outrageous conduct, but by maintaining their own faith and winning the argument."

If this is so, then the practising Christian continues to have a special responsibility to offer recommendations to those in authority, especially when there is such an obvious lack of standards by which to make decisions. Although we cannot expect the law of the land to be framed to facilitate Christian aspirations, we have, nevertheless, a responsibility to show how far Christian values can contribute to the well-being of the whole society. For example, when the evidence from history shows that immorality is associated with social decline, we must be prepared to campaign for high moral standards in the community. We should also be able to expect in a democracy that our views will receive consideration in proportion to our presence in the community.

The Christian must recognize that the standards which he demands of himself will be higher than those which society is prepared to demand or legislate for. There is an idealism, unmatched elsewhere, in the Christian's refusal to accept good when the best is available.

Nevertheless, in rather marked contrast to so much negative legislation defining what may **not** be done, the Christian has very clear positive lines of guidance concerning what is suitable and edifying.

> "Fill your minds with those things that are good and deserve praise: things that are true, noble, right, pure, lovely and honourable."[3]

In a general discussion of the extent to which Christian beliefs should contribute to society's standards, A.N. Triton[4] advocates that the principles outlined in the Ten Commandments should be brought before those in power:

> "The powers are organs of the law of God concerned to strengthen family life and respect for life, truth, and others' property, and so on. The Old Testament prophets, therefore, constantly demanded justice in employment and at law, honesty in trade, and purity in sexual life, as well as care for the weak, the overseas visitor, and the aged. They denounced luxury, exploitation, neglect of family loyalties and of the Sabbath."

A CHRISTIAN STANCE NEEDED

Other guidelines which would be consistent with Christian principles, but endorsed more widely also, would include the need to combat the powerful dehumanizing forces at work in our society. These forces are at work more broadly than simply in the media, of course; but, inasfar as the media provide a commentary on these influences, they can either facilitate them or combat them. It would be encouraging to see a film rejected because it dealt with the exploitation of people in such a way that exploitation seemed legitimate. A survey of violent films and cigarette advertising would show this theme to be a common feature.

Closely allied to this theme is the portrayal of alienation. The importance of this problem in contemporary society has been dealt with in recent years by the Marxist psychologist, Erich Fromm; but one finds it discussed by Durkheim already at the beginning of this century. In a thoughtful letter, Professor Julius Stone of Sydney has drawn attention to the contribution which the media have made to an increased acceptance of the alienated individual in a way which benefits neither the person nor society. He writes:

> "Durkheim pointed out in his pioneering sociological study of Le Suicide 73 years ago, that mass democracy, especially in its complex urban industrial concentrations, tended to increase the number of marginal individuals not capable of adjusting to participation and even survival in it. Such individuals typified the phenomenon of *anomie*, or social alienation. Durkheim's main observation of the increase of alienated individuals in mass societies

has been generally confirmed by later statistics. . . Instead of alienated individuals becoming isolated and disappearing one way or another from social life, they seem now to be acquiring a formidable cohesion of their own. By an extraordinary paradox, 'movements' of such 'alienated' individuals have become a steady feature of democratic societies. . . A main part of the responsibility for this may have to be placed on the voracious appetite of the mass media for the sensational, the abnormal, the violent, the iconoclastic, the cynical, the explosive, the hopeless, the disastrous, and (not least) the quaint though trivial topicality of the day. . . Is not the time overdue for us to recognize this irrelevance, and to expose the social evils which are sometimes shielded by claims of free expression? The enormous power of the media bids them accept responsibility also for the social consequences of its arbitrary exercise."[5]

One more general observation about criteria is worth making. Difficulty is often experienced about deciding what is **wrong** with a presentation, and words like "obscene", "corrupting", or "likely to deprave" are used. Too rarely is it asked, "What is **missing** that needs to be there?" Yet, in essence, the objections that are raised to such material as pornography often ask this question unwittingly. The objection lies in the presentation of physical acts **without** any relational aspect. Sexual encounters are represented **without** any thought of marriage; violence is inflicted **without** any consideration of consequences. It is this very detached presentation of such themes that lies behind the problems of alienation and dehumanization.

One further consideration in seeking standards is whether evidence of **exploitation** exists. Even those who try to present a "civil liberties" defence of pornography will commonly admit a dilemma here. While standing for the free choice of the consumer, they have to recognize that actors, models, and trade outlets are subject to a great deal of exploitation. In actual fact, of course, even the consumer is being exploited in that his appetite is pandered to only in exchange for very considerable financial outlay.

As the links between the pornography industry and organized crime are progressively exposed, so the extent to which exploitation is a close associate of pornography cannot be evaded. Reports from Denmark and America implicate the Mafia and other criminal groups in a great deal of the industry. Australians should therefore be concerned that, although there was little evidence of locally-produced pornography before 1970, it is now possible to screen a film which claims to feature the "thriving" industry in Australia.

RIGHTEOUSNESS EXALTS A NATION

These recommendations take us a long way away from the criterion of prevailing community standards. Essentially, the difference relates to sets of values. Any judgement based on prevailing standards, however exactly assessed, can only provide an assessment of what *is,* but it can say nothing about what *ought to be.* Even though it is a daunting task for anyone to establish laws based on values, it is not unreasonable to seek this. Indeed, simply to retain the laws of censorship which have sought to keep out the indecent and obscene would be to operate in terms of value-judgements. That these laws still exist should be our encouragement, and a challenge to have them enforced. Appendix 2 provides a summary of the relevant laws which should still be invoked.

The alternative is to make no value-judgements at all, but simply to gauge public reaction. This might appear as an unimpeachably neutral situation which is fair to all. In fact, however, as Professor Stone's letter makes clear, this apparent neutrality actually means accepting demands of the mass media. Since the media thrive on the abnormal and unusual, the recurrent presentation of such themes will **create** a set of community standards quite at variance with any standards that might be based on desirable values.

Essentially, the plea is made here for **quality control** in the materials available in our community. The concept of censorship may have negative overtones these days; the term quality control seeks to emphasize positive values.

We all recognize the need for manufacturers to use quality control procedures so that inferior products are rejected. We all expect food and water to be screened and filtered for impurities. Can we afford to ignore a similar approach to our community's moral and psychological diet?

The analogy can be developed further. Rejection of products is necessary sometimes because of impurities put in, and sometimes because of good things left out. In the same way, with books, films, and plays, we must carefully evaluate both what is said and what is not said.

11

A Basis For Advocating Control

Moral restraints should be built into legislation only if they concern society. Reasonable control, although restricting a few . . . will increase the freedom of the majority. *A.N. Triton*

In an ideal world there would be no call for a customs department, or any authority charged with the quality control of books, plays, and films. Ideally, people of all ages would be discriminating, selecting only what would be of benefit to them. The free availability of drugs and firearms would be no problem in a society where all could control their impulses without harming themselves or others. But just as the human species fails to avoid substances which will be physically damaging, so, too, his psychological appetite is warped. Just as people will smoke or drink themselves to death, so they will seek after the trivial or the bawdy more readily than quality entertainment. As we recognize the need to protect people from themselves by institutions such as the Drug Evaluation Committee, so we appear in need of an organization established to discriminate between the worthwhile and the dangerous in what we read and view. It is impractical to leave these decisions to unqualified people.

As things stand, we are in danger of being dictated to by the few who cannot even control themselves. Following the tragic killings at the 1972 Olympic Games in Munich, a Washington newspaper correspondent wrote:

> "The tragedy at the Olympic Games is just the latest reminder that there is now a kind of madness in the world, a lunatic strain of anarchy that hinders the peace and order of mankind . . . The majority exists with the tyranny of the minority. . . The problem is that the majority has not been able to devise ways of controlling the maniacal and even nonsensical acts of deranged agitators and dunderheads."

This comparison is more than just an analogy. "Maniac" was also the caption for a news-report of a 79-year-old woman in North Sydney who was murdered by someone who lacerated her repeatedly, hacked her with a mattock, sexually assaulted her, and left her with the mattock in her skull and a breadknife in her back.[1] Such a description bears an uncomfortable similarity to some of the contemporary sadistic pornography.

SELF-CONTROL IS UNRELIABLE

In the ideal society one could also expect the producers of mass entertainment to exercise responsible decisions about the quality of their products. The codes of acceptability, established by the film and publishing industries, in recent years seem to have developed remarkable elasticity in the face of financial pressures. Where the profit motive is strong, exploitation will occur unless curbed. As the censorship controls in Australia have been relaxed and liberalized, vested interests have not been slow in pushing a great wave of material irrespective of community effects.

It is inescapable that the responsibility for deciding what is in the community's interests lies with those appointed to the task. As things stand, this responsibility has been vested in politicians. It has been questioned above whether this is desirable, as political expediency may discourage unpopular but necessary legislation. In considering the extent to which controls can be exercised, it must be also recognized that there are limits beyond which the State can not, and should not, attempt to go.

Government cannot make men good; neither can it make them prosperous or happy. The evils in society are directly traceable to the vices of individual human beings. At its best, governments may simply attack the secondary manifestations of these vices. Their primary manifestations are found in the pride, covetousness, lust, envy, sloth, and plain incompetency of individual people.

GOVERNMENT CONTROL IS NECESSARY

It is important, then, to press for governments to act at the secondary level, while recognizing also that all members of the community must accept a share of the responsibility in deciding what shall be available.

"Society itself has a substantial say, both through legislation and through the pressures of public opinion, in determining the forms of behaviour that are permissible solutions to conflict and those that are not. . . Any society must recognize, therefore, that its decisions as to what it will sanction, and what it will prohibit, will be likely to have a powerful effect on the prevalence of the particular behaviour."[2]

Since all the most recent polls indicate that a majority of the population still favours some form of censorship, it is important to think responsibly about the ways censorship should operate, and why. There is no doubt that those who favour abolition of censorship have a thoroughly-reasoned position. Yet those who favour its retention have also put forward serious arguments. We may conclude, therefore, that such fundamentally-divergent viewpoints arise from different basic assumptions. These are of a philosophical or ideological nature. It is necessary to spell out a set of assumptions which might be adopted as a basis for advocating censorship as a means of social control over the quality of our mass media. Having done that, we may turn to some of the responses that have developed in Australia to the changes in moral and social values described above.

12

Some Fundamental Assumptions

I wonder if it is the case that the man who has the audacity to get up in any corrupt society and squarely preach justice or valour or the like always wins? — C.S. Lewis

Some have supposed that the defence of quality control arises from psychological presuppositions or evidence. The following pages will make clear that they are merely part of the evidence, and that one could expect other psychologists to disagree, not on the basis of the scientific data (which is debatable enough) but on quite different grounds. In reality, differences over the value or otherwise of controls stem from more fundamental considerations of the nature of society, the nature of man, attitudes to authority and to God.

The following assumptions are proposed as a basis for advocating some degree of quality control. In presenting them, every effort has been made to be true to the best scientific evidence. In addition, this evidence is interpreted from the standpoint of a Christian philosophy of man, which accepts his sinful nature and looks for guiding principles from the Bible.

Evidence from ethics must be accepted along with evidence from scientific studies, the latter being no more valid than the former. "Psychology is the study of behaviour" fairly states the appropriate area of enquiry for psychology. "Ethics is the study of behaviour"[1] with equal validity asserts that ethics is a study not of how we **do** behave, but how we **ought** to behave. The two are complementary.

In offering such a definition of ethics, it must be emphasized that ethical values have a source outside the man; they are derived from revelation by God, who is able to show how we ought to behave. This stance rejects the humanist view that moral values are derived from human experience, since a system based only on what is, or has been, cannot offer a future goal. The humanist can only say that he seeks the good life here and now; he lacks the discipline of constraint which comes from a recognition of God's plan for all mankind of all ages and cultures.

ASPECTS OF CHRISTIAN ETHICS

The Christian ethic of concern for others is widely rejected by many who are vocal for civil rights for the individual, but we must assume that mature adults recognize a responsibility to protect those unable to care for themselves. In principle, this view is still widely held in relation to children and the vulnerable, but the abolition of censorship would remove such protection.

The Christian ethic is concerned with human relationships. The preservation of human dignity and, in particular, respect for women, have long been identifying features of "Christian" societies. While censorship may be used either to enhance or to destroy human relationships, the present liberalization is leading to a distorted view of human relations; the abnormal is presented as normal, the violent as acceptable, the perverted as healthy, the trashy as desirable.

The Christian ethic also asserts "that I am not only responsible for the harm I have done, but that I am equally responsible for the harm I could have prevented".[1] This is **not** paternalism, or busybodying in the affairs of others; it is a high sense of social responsibility. It is too late to act with some measures of control after harmful or offensive material has been disseminated; the harm has been unleashed. Moderate censorship can provide reasonable safeguards to prevent such a situation.

The Christian ethic also has something to say concerning the proposition that the individual should be free to make his own choices, provided that these do not harm others, and that he is able to choose. Few will quibble with the first proviso; but let it be stressed that **all** the effects of choice must be reckoned with — not just the immediate consequences. Regarding the proviso of his ability to choose, there is the valid concern that our freedom has already been seriously impaired by those with financial and political axes to grind. Less censorship would simply erode this freedom.

Many intelligent and well-meaning people are adamant in opposition to any censorship of books on the ground that mature adults should be at liberty to make their own choice of reading-matter. Yet no such liberty has ever existed. The choice is made for us by publishers; they decide what books will be printed, primarily on commercial grounds. When an author submits a manuscript of real value and with high moral standards, a publisher may pass it over in favour of a book of dubious or low moral value because elements in the latter will promote high sales. The former manuscript is just as effectively censored by such decisions as by any formal method; but the way in which it occurs is much more difficult to challenge on rational grounds.

ETHICS AND THE PRESS

Similarly, newspaper editors commonly resist any form of censorship, proclaiming the virtues of "freedom of the press". All too often this means freedom for the editor to print what will sell the paper. A balanced presentation of the news cannot really be expected from any one paper; but the bias of one can hopefully be offset by the different policy or outlook of another. The situation, however, can be very dangerous when (as in Australia) the media are controlled by so few people.

This problem has been discussed at some length by Nichols, who writes, "The extraordinary situation has arisen in Australia that four monopolies owned or controlled each by a single family now control almost the entire mass communications network. . . Proprietorial control of undertakings so big or so entrenched that competition is effectively ruled out, is obviously potentially dangerous. . . The vastly improved news and information services all over the world have brought a flood of news and views which editorial staffs have to sift through and censor because of inevitable limitations of space. . . Predetermined editorial policy on any issue will obviously have the result of censoring out items which contravene that policy. Thus the public no longer hears the alternative view."[2]

True freedom of the press implies a balanced presentation of the news and the views of all sectors of society. Because of this, attempts to suppress the evidence of harm from pornography and the portrayal of violence are so dangerously dishonest.

THE ISSUE OF FREEDOM

The stance of this writer is based on the assumption that, given complete freedom to choose, people will tend to select the bad rather than the good. This view derives from a Christian doctrine of man, and conflicts sharply with the unreal optimism of humanism. History gives little support to the view that man gets better and better as he exercises his choices without constraint. The Bible gives every reason to predict that, without God, man will sink lower and lower.

Until now, in Western society, it has not been possible to demonstrate the truth of this, since the law embodied moral principles so broadly. Now, as changes occur in which the law moves away from moral principles, we are beginning to see individuals and societies veering out of control — quite contrary to humanist expectations.

Of those who seriously seek unrestricted freedom for philosophical reasons, Maddison writes, "One may have nothing but admiration for those people who firmly maintain that there should be unrestricted freedom of publication, of film and theatrical performances, and so on, yet still believe they are wrong, even if this is for the best possible reasons — because of a singularly high-minded belief in the judgement and stability of the average human being — because they grossly underestimate the prevalence of serious neurotic conflicts in a contemporary Western population. They are in the best liberal tradition, and not necessarily impelled by neurotic motives — though on the other hand there are good reasons for believing that some of them are".[3]

Moreover, while the intellectual is clamouring for freedom to choose, the average man-in-the-street has neither the intellectual resources nor the inclination to make selective choices for himself and his family. However regrettable this may be, until it proves otherwise, it lies with those in authority to assist him.

The issue today is no longer related to the availability of high quality literature. The real issues have now shifted to the other end of the scale. The holes of the net may once have been too small for the literary genius to get through; now they are so large that trash, superficiality, and pornography can slip through too readily. Benjamin Spock has seen what many have yet to realize: "For decades I was an uncompromising civil libertarian and scorned the hypocrisy involved in the enforcement of obscenity laws. But recent trends in movies, literature, and art toward what I think of as shock obscenity, and the courts' acceptance of it, have made me change my position . . . particularly in view of other brutalizing trends".[4]

The critical decisions regarding what shall be admitted under existing regulations therefore depend less and less on the academic opinions of specialists in literature. It is not a question of artistic sensibilities being outraged, but of people's fundamental adjustments being irretrievably harmed. It is therefore valuable that the Commonwealth Film Board includes a psychiatrist. Yet the National Literature Board of Review lacks this provision. Psychological or psychiatric insights should be invariable components of any judgements on the effects of the kind of literature currently considered for entry. Other difficulties with these Federal boards have been discussed by Campbell and Whitmore.[5]

THE ISSUE OF PROGRESSIVE DECLINE

It is assumed further that, as one descends into poor quality literature, so public taste will deteriorate, leading to a demand for more explicit and more perverted material. The trend in books and films overseas and in this country confirms this. For example, in Copenhagen the trade in "sex objects" has now overtaken the sales of literature in the porn shops. In Washington at Christmas, the younger teenage market bought "grisly 'hobby-kit' toys with scantily-clad female plastic dolls provided for maiming and dismembering in toy torture chambers . . ."[6]

The decline into blatantly-destructive "entertainment" is well illustrated by the film, "The Exorcist". Widely condemned by responsible psychiatrists as a deadly mixture of sex, violence, and evil, which will pull young people down to a primitive level, it continues to be screened to capacity-audiences. Psychiatric research has been started in Pittsburgh because of the high incidence of breakdown following viewing of the film. Yet the film's director sees it as "a stepping stone which will give the studios courage to handle more ambitious themes with more graphic scenes".[7] It is a tragically irresponsible thing to collaborate with this lemming-like approach to collective self-destruction.

By this approach, once-shocking material loses its impact and will be replaced by more shocking material. Fantasy carries over into reality, and our reactions can be blunted as the Stoic Epictetus knew well:

> "Begin, he says, with a torn robe or a broken cup or plate, and say, 'I don't care'. Go on to the death of a pet dog or horse, and

say, 'I don't care'. In the end, you will come to a stage when you can stand beside the bed of your loved one and see that loved one die, and say, 'I don't care'." [8]

This progressive acceptance of what was previously traumatic is a most powerful principle. It is often used as a form of therapy known as "systematic desensitization" with impressive results. Eysenck[9] has described how films and television are peculiarly appropriate in achieving desensitization. Violence, horror, shock, and obscenity are presented to the viewer in a setting where he is able to feel comfortable and detached. He can switch off (physically or mentally) whenever he wishes, so levels of shock need never become more than is desired. Eventually the real horrors of war, death, and poverty become conversation-pieces, while the fantasy material of films is increasingly accepted with ease. This is not strictly brainwashing, but it has all the elements of powerful attitude-change.

DEPICTION PRODUCES ACTION

It must be recognized that it is impossible to keep various deviate practices simply at the level of literature or art. If we accept that group-sex is a fit subject for widely-available literature, we must anticipate a demand that the corresponding behaviour shall also be accepted within the community. One cannot indefinitely feed fantasy without this leading to overt behaviour. Just as homosexual themes in films and on TV have led to a wider acceptance of homosexual behaviour, so we need only look to the current themes of sadism and violence to realize what will be tomorrow's reality.

Similarly, with the portrayal of explicit sexual themes, it is obvious that the outcome of savouring the themes in fantasy will be the desire to experiment. What pornography promises, prostitution delivers. An upsurge of massage parlours has been the close sequel of the opening of sex shops. The rise in venereal disease to new levels is also a predictable outcome.

This objection to certain types of material assumes that there is some which is harmful. The border-line may be as difficult to judge as the line between pass and fail in an exam, but the two types are broadly recognizable. That absolute criteria are difficult or impossible does not mean that no discrimination should be attempted. We set up standards of quality control for food, commercial products, drugs; it seems logical to exercise similar care over psychologically-significant commodities. Indeed, even D.H. Lawrence, whose works have often broken new ground on the basis of literary merit, is clear enough in condemnation of pornography:

> "Even I would censor genuine pornography, rigorously. It would not be very difficult. . . You can recognize it by the insult it offers, invariably, to sex, and to the human spirit. Pornography is the attempt to insult sex, to do dirt on it. This is unpardonable. . . The insult to the human body, the insult to a vital human relationship! Ugly and cheap they make the human nudity, ugly and degraded they make the sexual act, trivial and cheap and nasty." [10]

Those who claim that the lines are hard to draw, rarely mention that lines have been drawn for many years according to legally-defined criteria. Difficulties have arisen, not only because the criteria were vague, but often because of determined attacks on them by those who were committed to the abolition of standards.

It must be stressed that the issue of censorship is not simply concerned with sex. The dangers of continued exposure to representations of violence, especially where it is approved or condoned, has been referred to above. It is often argued that the theatre must deal with the realities of life, and that violence is therefore a legitimate theme. This is, of course, true; but it is not a sufficient reply to the objection that those with aggressive tendencies will have them further aroused. It was once the clear convention of films that good must be shown to triumph over evil. Perhaps there is wisdom in seeking a return to that convention, since the most recent good evidence shows that "if the witnessed violence is regarded as 'wrong' or unjustified, many observers will restrain their aggressive inclinations for at least a brief period of time".[11]

Similarly, we are in danger of being swamped with superficial trash on bookstalls, and beguiled by misleading advertising of commercial products. It is the responsibility of those who seek change to prove it will not cause harm. To allow, in the name of freedom, the stimulation of every perverse fantasy of the disturbed, and the thoughtless wallowing of an uncritical public, can only harm the individual people and the community in which they live. In the long run, the prevailing trend for lowered standards of social values will threaten the freedom of minority and majority alike, as well as all regard for the personal welfare and safety of others. What price freedom then?

HOPE FOR OUR SOCIETY

It is assumed that the society in which we live has many faults and problems; but seeking to destroy that society is no solution. There is a hope springing out of the Christian ethic which believes that God can act in a corrupt society. It is not good enough to say Christianity has failed; it has not been seriously tried. For many years, our society has experienced the underpinning influences of Christian values; as a result, it has been cushioned from the worst effects of relaxation of standards. This cannot be expected to continue in our increasingly-secular society.

The call for freedom from all restraints (or "permissiveness") often arises from experiences in childhood and adolescence. In particular, an abdication of responsibility for decision-making by many intelligent parents (whose children are now of student-age) has meant that the phase of "testing-the-limits" is still unresolved. Many students are questioning parental values as inconsistent and hypocritical. This reaction is being generalized to a rejection of all forms of control by authority figures.

More than one generation of parents has been influenced by what Dr. Benjamin Spock appeared to advocate in his best seller, "Baby and Child Care". What has not always been realized is that he was reacting against an inhumane and rigid form of child-rearing which treated feeding and toilet-training procedures as more important than the baby. He advocated a more humane approach; but this greater flexibility has since been taken to ridiculous extremes, which he never intended and now clearly regrets. Dr. Spock now makes clear that many parents have abandoned their proper role as guides and guardians with disastrous consequences for parents and children alike.

PERMISSIVE OR SUBMISSIVE?

In an interview he expressed his dislike of the term "permissiveness" and showed that "submissiveness" would be a more suitable alternative. Asked why it is that some children are impossible behaviour-problems, he responded: "They are produced by submissiveness on the part of parents; and I distinguish between 'permissive' and 'submissive'. The word 'permissive' is dangerous . . . everyone has a different idea of where it begins. Submissive parents don't feel entitled to respect from a child. There is a guiltiness toward their children that makes them afraid to ask for respect. But if you don't set limits for a child, he'll keep pushing and pushing until he becomes obnoxious and the parent loses his patience and lands on him like a ton of bricks. Then the parent is overwhelmed by a sense of guilt and becomes submissive all over again."[12]

This rejection of authority has been planted in children's minds for long enough now for some of the adult world to propagate an anti-authority viewpoint in so extreme a way that it lacks rationality. Education is used as a political tool to subvert children's relationships to their parents: one way of achieving this is by the advocacy of explicit sex education. Huntford, Scandinavian correspondent of "The Observer", has studied the Swedish system, and refers to the philosophy of sex education there: "We have no ethical standards in education, and no rules for sexual behaviour. We don't care at what age children start going to bed with each other as long as they are prepared. Rules mean repression. And repression of sex leads to aggression."[13]

Such a view is sadly at odds with the psychological and sociological evidence. It could only be put forward by those who are intent on the destruction of the relationships which enable families and societies to survive.

THE WHOLE SPECTRUM IS INVOLVED

We can **not** assume that censorship alone will solve problems. If tried without other changes, the worst fears of the critics of censorship will be realized. The issues lie deeper and are more complex, as should be clear from earlier chapters. All the restless searching for satisfaction through hedonism, sex, drugs, and violence proves self-defeating. What starts as an attempt at self-actualization ends as a form of escape.

It remains for those who cannot accept these assumptions to re-examine their own and to respond accordingly. It is imperative that those who are in sympathy with this expressed viewpoint should stand up and be counted. That way we may begin to know what the prevailing community standards really are.

13

Raising the Standard

What is at stake is civilization and humanity, nothing less. The matter of pornography and obscenity is not a trivial one, and only superficial minds can take a bland and untroubled view of it. Irving Kristol

Not everyone is convinced that it is necessary to become involved in the moral state of society. Many of sincere Christian conviction believe there are strong reasons for remaining aloof from such issues. Among those who see the need, there are major differences about how the challenge should be met. Those who stress the need to deal with issues at the personal level are criticized for failing to respond to the broader social context within which people live. An involvement in the political or social welfare arena may be rejected by others as failing to deal with the issue at the fundamental level of personal change.

If a stand against an evil is taken, there are always many ready to attack this as "negative", though it is rarely explained why a stand against evil is really so dreadful. Implicitly, however, it is assumed that a stand against evil means taking a judgemental attitude also against people — a quite false assumption which does little credit to those who take this stance.

It will often be necessary to take a "negative" stand if ever positive advances are to be achieved. The architect of a tall building knows he must dig deep down if his building is to remain solid. In contemporary society, the foundations show signs of corruption; fine aspirations for the future will be useless unless we take a firm — and, if necessary, unpopular — stand against all that would undermine both individuals and society.

NONE CAN BE NEUTRAL

It is not possible to remain neutral on the changing standards in society today. Even though "right" and "wrong" should be matters of morality based on clear principles, in reality we face a situation where decisions are based on the supposed majority opinion. This is contrary to the true basis of morality; to ignore this is to take a stand which will strengthen the trend. Writing of the Christian's responsibility in this, Moberg says:

"It is impossible not to take sides in a democratic society: neutrality supports the side of whoever wins in the struggle for power. Sometimes that side may be consistent with Christian values: more often it will support vested interests sustained by wealth, power, and privileged position. 'Neutral' Christians thereby indirectly communicate that they believe those vested interests are morally right in social controversies."[1]

Moberg makes it clear that the contemporary challenge to Christians to be involved in matters of social concern is no new thing. It is not that Christians must now for the first time intervene in an area from which they have previously kept away. Rather the call is to **stop withdrawing** from involvement, which has until now provided a balance and stability to society which is rapidly being lost. If the established traditions of trust and integrity are lost, a democratic life-style must inevitably move towards either anarchy or totalitarianism. This fear has been brought sharply into focus by the events of Watergate. There the whole world has seen what can happen to a democracy when the fundamental assumptions about its leaders are undermined. Trust has been a basic assumption of Christian teaching, and an essential element in the establishment of a democratic life-style. Doubts over leadership have been mixed with a philosophy of personal autonomy in America to the extent that responsibility and concern for others has fallen to a low ebb. A bleak future is prophesied if decisions continue to rest on the raucous pressures of self-seeking pressure-groups. Jeremy Campbell, writing from Washington, has noted how the optimistic political philosophers are now having to rethink the future for America; other countries do well to learn from the struggles of Watergate. He writes:

". . . The cult of individual freedom implicit in the glories of the European Renaissance and the founding of the American republic is now tearing the necessary bonds of society asunder, spreading psychological havoc and imposing on ordinary citizens a new kind of serfdom they can scarcely recognize, let alone control . . . Strong authoritarian governments may be 'unavoidable, even necessary' if the West is to survive the enormous strains and conflicts of the next decades. . . The trouble is that just when democracy has come of age, we are giving enormous power to pressure-groups. We have come to accept the idea that if no rational answers can be found, policy will be decided on the basis of whoever squawks the loudest, whoever has the capacity to make things messy."[2]

Invariably, pressures in society bring about a response which serves in some measure as a check or balance to what may otherwise represent a danger. When governments move too far towards the right or the left, contrary forces operate to bring a more moderate influence. When a society becomes generally repressive, a reaction occurs to champion individual freedom. Conversely, when a libertarian influence goes too far, there comes a demand for a return to controls. All of this might sound like a healthy and natural cycle of events, requiring little involvement from the individual citizen other than patiently waiting for the swing of the pendulum. Unfortunately, three considerations make it necessary to take a more active part in shaping the future.

DON'T RELY ON THE PENDULUM

First, the pressures towards a decline in moral standards are not being engineered for the good of society. There is big money to be made from corruption, so that to remain impassive is to condone exploitation. Secondly, this move towards corruption is associated with an amoral view of life which cares nothing for those who would be hurt by the prevailing trends. Simply to wait for a swing of the pendulum to correct existing evils takes no account of the inestimable harm to many, especially young people, who suffer meantime. Thirdly, allowing a trend to go to a foolish extreme provokes a reaction which is as unhealthy as that which it seeks to counter. How sad it would be if we have to wait for "permissiveness" to go so far that a Victorian type of repression takes its place. How very much better to be party to a more moderate force which does not seek simply to counter the present, nor press for a return to the past, but can constructively work towards a future where the principles of morality are clearly understood and implemented in a balanced way.

Such a move would not be reactionary; it would not be repressive. It would certainly be a stand against declining personal and public morality. But its aim would be to raise the standard.

Raising the standard is a symbolic act in a military campaign. It implies that the battle is on against opposing forces. The changing standards of recent years have brought just such a response over the last few years. Numerous groups, small and large, have come into being to take issue with various social and legislative changes. To those involved in them, they have been of vital significance, and often very effective.

The **Right to Life Association** is an example of a successful rallying of concerned citizens throughout Australia in the face of strong pressures to make abortion widely available. The movement was not sufficiently well-organized to counter efforts to change the law in South Australia; but, learning from that experience, it showed what could be done when similar legislation came before the Federal Parliament in Canberra. The strength of that movement has been its ability to present facts relevant to the issue, and to mobilize public support. It has also demonstrated the reality of its intention to show true love by its sacrificial provision of facilities for girls who choose against abortion. It has, in other words, not only stood *against* abortion, but *for* life. It has attracted men and women of competence and integrity to lead others. The suggestion that the organization is only Catholic-supported is quite unjustified. Certainly the Catholic Church has given a lead and support throughout which has been entirely consistent with its teaching; but many others have been able to understand the issues and to lend support to what is a matter of morality irrespective of religious persuasion. As the pro-abortionists continue to press their claims, so it becomes increasingly evident that "freedom of personal choice" and the "right of a child to be wanted" serve as little more than catch-cries. There is an almost fascistic pressure towards euthanasia and infanticide, as well as more widespread abortion, which would override the principles of those who see things differently. Freedom to choose too easily becomes only freedom to agree with a pressure-group. Freedom of conscience for the doctor or nurse receives as little consideration as does the right of the unborn child.

Various other groups with fairly specific aims have emerged. Usually beginning with a basis in Christian morality, they incorporate a wider appeal to creation ethics and seek the support of all concerned citizens. Most have been local, but some have achieved national co-ordination. In Queensland, a group has emerged to make a special issue of pornography and the quality of literature prescribed for use in places of education. Under the title, **Society to Outlaw Pornography** (STOP), it has circulated information around Australia, as well as operating as a small but vocal pressure-group within the State.

In South Australia, a similar reaction to the quality of advertising provoked the advent of the **Council to Stop Offensive Advertising.** By acting as a clearing-house for complaints from those who have been offended, it has the characteristics of a consumer-protection organization. Inevitably, much of its activity (as with STOP) is against what people report as unacceptable, but it also seeks to give positive support to those advertisers who maintain high standards. For example, it maintains a "white list" of advertisers who are commended because of their scrupulous standards of advertising. Members are kept advised of the list, and, of course, give their patronage accordingly.

Television has been another area where standards have caused alarm, especially among parents. This has led to active groups developing in Victoria and in South Australia (ACTAC — **Australian Childrens Television Action Committee**). In addition to educating parents and others to the potential hazards and benefits of television, these committees have carried out a commendable amount of original work, producing reports both for government and for general circulation. Such unselfish, and yet socially-valuable, activity provides a good example of what truly-responsible democracy can achieve when people who care use the resources open to them.

On a slightly broader base, the **Community Standards Organisation** (CSO) has been active in most Australian States for a number of years. It has been directed to the influences of the media generally, taking a stand on films and pornographic literature in particular. Branches in all States have operated as autonomous units, with an informal national organization to co-ordinate ideas and action. It has produced material in the form of a newsletter to inform members and others of current trends in Australia and overseas. It has operated largely as a consciousness-raising group, seeking to alert citizens and inform parliamentarians. One of its pamphlets which has received wide distribution is called "You and the Permissive Society". This is reproduced as Appendix 3, as it incorporates a number of other helpful suggestions for the responsible citizen.

ACTION ON SPECIFIC ISSUES

From time to time it has taken action on specific issues which have appeared to be test-cases. The most widely-publicized was the injunction taken out by the Moral Action Committee of South Australia (which later merged with CSO) against the staging of the play "Oh! Calcutta!". The success of this action was for Australia as much a watershed event as was the failure to stop the show in London. The whole action has been recorded in the book, "No, No, Calcutta"[3], with a careful explanation of why such a step proved necessary. Those who so readily attack such action as if it were forcing the opinions of the few on the many, would do well to read the account and to note how the enforcement of law is a necessary aspect of community life. The CSO has no power to force anyone to do anything, but it can and does act as a catalyst for public opinion and law enforcement.

Numerous other actions have been successfully undertaken in the years since, including an interim injunction against the film version of "Oh! Calcutta!" when it was to be screened in South Australia in 1973. Again, the principle of enforcement of existing laws was at stake, and the CSO in that State gained a favourable decision. This decision was subsequently reversed by the Supreme Court in June 1974, not because the validity of the original decision was questioned, but because of a subsequent change in the law. By an alteration to the "R" certificate legislation, it was made impossible for citizens to challenge a Federal decision if the responsible Minister or his nominee should view a film and approve its certificate. This law came into force in April 1974, and was used by the South Australian Premier, Mr. Don Dunstan, to permit the showing of "Oh! Calcutta!". Two odd features of this changed decision can be noted. The Premier himself did not sign the certificate of approval, nor was his nominee a person from South Australia — as could reasonably have been expected in a decision taken by the State in relation to a Federal ruling. This mode of action calculatedly ignored the intention of this legislation that the States should preserve the right to make local decisions.

In giving his decision in the Supreme Court, Mr. Justice Walters said he agreed with the earlier decision of Mr. Justice Sangster in 1973 that "the exhibition of this film would be the exhibition of indecent matter". The amending legislation had the effect of overriding the provisions of the Police Offences Act, and Mr. Justice Walters had no alternative but to dissolve the injunction. In doing so, he said, "I will proffer the opinion that the film is devoid of artistic merit, is dreary, dull and wearisome, and will throw slush at members of the public who will be moved to see it. . . Though we live in a society of changing standards of outlook and behaviour, there does exist in our community — however the standards may vary from time to time — a general instinctive sense of what is decent and what is indecent, of what is clean and what is dirty. Some may think that the feelings of people who have a sensitivity in matters of decency and good taste are entitled to be respected just as much as those of the vociferous minority who, in the name of freedom, shout for ugliness in all its forms."

On a national basis, the CSO has co-ordinated action on a number of issues relating to books, films, and television. It has acted through representations to governments, public meetings, press statements, production of books, and a quarterly information journal, as well as by helping individuals to play an active part in shaping community standards. Predictably, a great deal of criticism and hostile reporting from many directions has sought to undermine the image of the organization. However, remarkably few of the critics have taken the trouble to make personal contact with those they criticize. Perhaps the most persistently misguided and ill-informed attacks have come through the Adelaide journalist, Max Harris. His exaggerations and innuendoes have no doubt had a plausibility for those who assume that he writes with some degree of evidence behind him. It is therefore worth recording that the only consistency he has demonstrated over the years has been his refusal to come face-to-face with those whom he attacks most. Criticizing from a position of ignorance and isolation in this way is as easy as the dismissing of the theories of nuclear physics would be for a boy who failed to pass matriculation in that area.

THE FESTIVAL OF LIGHT

The CSO has also been responsible, with other groups, notably the Australian Evangelical Alliance, for the establishment of the **Australian Festival of Light** (AFOL). Following the outstanding success of the Festival of Light in Britain in bringing matters of morality into public focus, the need for a similar movement was recognized early in 1972.

The Australian FOL has emerged since that time as a significant force representing the hopes and aspirations of very many people. Its beginnings in South Australia and the eastern States were marked by a great deal of quiet planning so that it was a year before any public activity occurred. The visit of Cliff Richard to Australia on a singing tour for The Evangelical Alliance Relief (TEAR) Fund provided a suitable occasion to present the positive emphasis that was envisaged. Cliff Richard spoke and sang of the part which he had played in the British Festival, giving many throughout Australia a vision of what could be achieved. As he sang to capacity crowds, he gained the attention of whole families, and especially of young people.

From the beginning there was a clear emphasis on the importance of the family-unit in society — not just the nuclear-family, but the broader unit involving the wide range of family relationships wherever they exist. This emphasis has remained as a central principle, determining the issues which command the attention of the Festival; its importance for individuals and for the good of society has been affirmed both on an ethical basis and in more pragmatic terms.

Opponents have repeatedly tried to represent the Festival in other ways. Projecting it as "anti-porn" and "anti-sex" has been a convenient, but misguided, shorthand for abuse. A firm stand against pornography has, of course, been a feature of Festival statements, for pornography is so blatantly anti-family; but the deeper issues underlying demand for pornography have been properly emphasized. This together with a "pro-sex" emphasis is evident in the following:

"'Guilt and fear are not dispelled by pornography: on the contrary, it encourages us to enjoy hate in our attitudes to sex and to have contempt for other people, especially women'. . . It should, then, be clear that a stand against pornography expresses a view that sexuality is something good and special. It springs from a high view of personal relationships which seeks to respect the dignity and personal worth of others. If so, then it follows we must do **more** than simply be concerned about widespread availability of pornography.

"Both demand from consumers, and growing acceptance in the community, should direct our attention to the deep and unsatisfied needs which are proliferating. There is a sense in which the control of pornography is to remove the fruits of a plant while leaving the roots to thrive. If we recognize that pornography means hate, we shall do well to find ways to counter the development of hate. The Christian message of love runs directly counter to this, and would explain why so many people react against pornography even though they are not sure why. If we take our caring seriously, we will not react simply against those outward expressions which offend us personally, but will want to find ways to reduce the emotional distress which finds its expression in this distorted material." [4]

After the first launching of the Festival around Australia in May 1973, developments soon led to the visit of Mrs. Mary Whitchouse for speaking engagements in many parts of the country in late 1973. The media took a great interest in her visit, and gave her coverage even before she left Britain. Her reputation as an effective speaker and clear thinker had been recognized by her supporters and her critics alike. Repeated efforts to discredit her efforts for the National Viewers and Listeners Association in Britain had failed,[5] and the Australian media were obviously keen to have their try.

She spoke first in Darwin and found an unexpectedly large and receptive audience. Industrial troubles were disturbing air-traffic at the time, so that the remainder of her journey was in constant danger of disruption. After speaking in Brisbane she found that the airlines had discontinued service just as she was due to fly on to Sydney for a major press conference. A light plane was chartered, and, after a hair-raising and lengthy journey, she belatedly confronted the press for several hours.

The next two weeks of public speaking presented a gruelling time-table, enough to tax the resources of the strongest person. That she had been severely ill prior to arrival and quite unable to speak for several months was known to few. Her stamina and good humour were, therefore, the more remarkable. A large meeting at the university in Canberra was followed by a rally in Sydney which caused the Town Hall, St. Andrews Cathedral, and the Lyceum Theatre all to overflow.

Enthusiasm and support developed rapidly from these events, and led to major meetings in Tamworth, Adelaide, and Melbourne. Wide interest was generated by her appearance on "Monday Conference" on ABC television, where, with the Rev. Lance Shilton, she confronted a humanist opponent on the issue of censorship. So successful was this encounter that the next issue of the "Australian Humanist" lamented, "Why don't humanists do their homework?"[6] In predictably hostile fashion, that article remarked that "Mary Whitehouse and Lance Shilton, stupid and all as they are, had Ken Horler reduced to invective and insult on 'Monday Conference'." Further rather incoherent abuse littered that issue of the journal, and strongly suggested that the Festival of Light was not something to be ignored. Confrontation over facts and opinion has continued in that journal; the presuppositions of libertarianism must be continuously challenged.[7]

The high-points of the Festival's activities in October 1973 undoubtedly occurred in Adelaide.

Preparatory activity resulted in the establishment of Light groups, meeting in many suburbs for weeks before. Literature was produced by way of information and exhortation. Notably, this included a well-produced magazine entitled "Light", and a small book written to alert people to the need to become more personally involved in shaping the values of society.[8]

A whole series of activities culminated in functions for all age-groups. The family emphasis was apparent in: a kite-flying contest (Festival of Flight); a "Focus on Youth" concert; a women's rally at the newly-opened Adelaide Festival Theatre; and a march and rally for all ages, which attracted over 12,000 people. On this last occasion, in addition to an address by Mary Whitehouse, a detailed proclamation was announced from which extracts were read. This statement clearly indicated the breadth of concern of the Festival (see Appendix 4). It received almost no attention from the press, except for the "Southern Cross", although it contained many specific and constructive recommendations.

The developing interest of this movement and its range of involvement was recognized as a whole series of radio and TV programs was presented, featuring various members of the Festival across Australia, in which the FOL stand was examined.

Efforts to polarize opinion resulted in sharp antagonism from some people, both from within the Churches and from outside. The idea that groups in the community might make a stand on moral issues was challenged; the spectre of manipulative and repressive forces was often invoked. In actual fact, this latter fear, though perhaps justified in anticipation, has not been confirmed. A continuing program, with allegiance from a very wide range of political and church opinion, has developed.

A fair and dispassionate account of events to the end of 1973 was published by Hilliard and Warhurst.[9] As independent observers writing with academic care, they reported, with special emphasis on South Australia, that "the AFOL is a more significant movement than many of those outside it will allow. . . Any organization which mobilizes the numbers which the AFOL has so far succeeded in attracting is not to be lightly dismissed".

BY AUSTRALIANS FOR AUSTRALIA

Following the initiative provided by the visit of Mary Whitehouse, the Festival of Light has proceeded to establish an essentially-Australian image. Leadership from elsewhere is valued, but cannot replace active involvement at the grass-roots level by those living in contemporary Australia. Further rallies, marches, and published material have, therefore, stressed the importance of many people playing a part rather than the reliance on the charisma of a small band of leaders.

The emphasis on what is good and suitable for families was apparent at a concert in the Sydney Opera House, when a largely-musical program featured a dramatic presentation, "Lightshine". Similarly, an exciting development has been the music of a singing group from Sydney, known as the Young World Singers, who have travelled widely and promoted the Festival by their singing. Their recording of "Light Up the Fire" has been popular with all ages. A Brisbane group, Family, has also provided musical support at many big rallies. The effectiveness of this musical approach has been most obvious in large rallies in Canberra and Launceston early in 1974.

Out of the desire to promote what is good has come a strong development in the entertainment area. As a very practical answer to those critics who suggest that moralists are joyless "wowsers", Australian Family Entertainment Promotions (AFEP) has emerged through the initiatives of the New South Wales FOL. Indications from America were that when good films are screened in a locality they receive support from thankful families. Following this lead, AFEP took a bold step in inviting the Pat Boone family to Australia for a ten-day tour. The group, together with the Young World singers, toured early in 1975 with outstanding success. A new record was created at the Sydney Opera House; four successive performances were booked out. The choice was an appropriate one since not only was the ideal of happy family life projected visibly, but Pat Boone has for a long time been associated with a stand for better quality entertainment in America. The indications are that the trend towards more wholesome entertainment will receive widespread support in other countries, too, where many have grown sick of their loss of freedom of choice.

The importance of a broadly-based response to changing community standards became obvious at the start of 1974 as several pieces of legislation were brought forward in Federal Parliament dealing with issues already espoused by the Festival of Light. An earlier attempt to introduce divorce law reform was reintroduced under the title of The Family Law Bill. Concurrently, The Human Rights Bill was introduced, based ostensibly on the Universal Declaration of Human Rights.

ACTION IN THE POLITICAL ARENA

There was widespread reaction to both Bills, and the Festival played an active part in drawing public attention to the more controversial clauses of both Bills. Well researched documents were produced to identify the more unacceptable features of the Bills. A great deal of coverage was given to the omission of Article 16(3) in the Universal Declaration which states that "the family is the natural and fundamental group-unit of society and is entitled to protection by society and the State". (Article 21(1) of the International Covenant on Civil and Political Rights).

Efforts to speed these Bills through Parliament were frustrated by a double dissolution. A Federal election in May 1974 gave a further focus for action in reminding electors of their responsibility to take account of moral issues in their voting. This emphasis was notably present at the April rally in Sydney which was the culmination of a week of education and information. An ambitious program of events, under the general supervision of the Rev. Fred Nile, full-time FOL director in New South Wales, attracted wide attention. The final rally in Hyde Park attracted some 35,000 participants — an event it would be difficult to disregard. Nevertheless "The Australian" succeeded in misrepresenting the occasion by referring to an attendance of 2,500 people! The error was in the predictable direction; as often happens with such errors, this told more of the newspaper than it did of the event.

That rally was chaired by the New South Wales Minister for Transport, the Hon. Milton Morris. The range of speakers included Cardinal Freeman of the Catholic Church, and the Anglican Archbishop Marcus Loane. A wide representation from other Churches and professional groups once again demonstrated a breadth of support for the Festival platform. A clear challenge to the Government to take a responsible stand on moral issues was presented by the Dean of Sydney, The Very Rev. Lance Shilton, while the Rev. Alan Walker stressed that the Festival was not aligned with or against any one political party. This was most necessary as various efforts had been made to identify the Festival with the political right-wing.

This point was made even more clearly in the Melbourne rally a few weeks later. On that occasion, speakers were chosen with a careful attention to the political spectrum. Mr. Jim Beggs, a waterside worker clearly identified with the political left, spoke of "The Family — Keystone of Society", while the Liberal Senator, Ivor Greenwood Q.C., spoke on "Community Standards". Poised politically somewhere between these two, the present author spoke on "Pornography, Violence, and Hate".

A feature of that rally was a telegram sent by the-then Governor-General, Sir Paul Hasluck, and read on his behalf by Sir Edmund Herring (known to most Australians for his famous "Call to the Nation"). The telegram read:

> PLEASE CONVEY TO ALL THOSE TAKING PART IN THE AUSTRALIAN FESTIVAL OF LIGHT MY GOOD WISHES FOR THE SUCCESS OF THEIR MEETING IN MELBOURNE. AT THIS TIME OF CONFLICTING STANDARDS THE AUSTRALIAN PEOPLE, ESPECIALLY THE YOUNGER GENERATION, LOOK FOR GUIDANCE AND LEADERSHIP, AND FACE THE NEED FOR EDUCATION IN THOSE VALUES ON WHICH A GOOD SOCIETY RESTS. AS GOVERNOR GENERAL I GIVE MY FULL SUPPORT TO YOUR CONSTRUCTIVE EFFORTS TO UPHOLD THE BEST

STANDARDS OF PUBLIC AND PERSONAL CONDUCT AND TO PROMOTE AMONG ALL AUSTRALIANS THE SEARCH FOR WHAT IS GOOD AND TRUE.

As election campaigning continued, the various branches of the Festival of Light examined ways of being the kind of influence which true democratic responsibility demands. In South Australia, Senate candidates were canvassed for their views on a wide range of moral issues, and the position of each party was given publicity. In New South Wales, it was feared that strongly anti-family candidates might be successful in gaining a Senate seat; consequently, at the eleventh hour, three members of the FOL Committee, headed by Mrs. Frieda Brown, campaigned independently as the Family Action Movement. With little money and less time, this trio attracted a quite amazingly-high vote. This vote for the family must be seen as a significant sign of support remaining in the community for the protection of marriage and the family against those forces tending to erode them. Indeed, the vote of 68,561 is a clearer indication of real interest, at a level which counts, than such indicators as attendance at meetings and rallies. Even though the challenge is not basically one of who has the numbers, but rather where lie right and wrong, it is true that for a community-based movement to be taken seriously it must be able to demonstrate widespread support.

READY FOR FURTHER ACTION

AFOL and the other organizations mentioned in this chapter continue to be active. Only the first phases can be recorded at this stage. They are all of recent origin, and represent the response to changing standards. All, in their respective areas, are seeking to raise the standard. That all have experienced opposition indicates, on the one hand, that they have been proving effective; on the other hand, criticism indicates that some mistakes have also been made. This is predictable in so precarious an area, but is no reason to abdicate responsibility.

Behind the thousands who have publicly supported these standard-raising groups are many more thousands who, though unwilling to be identified, are grateful for what has been attempted.

Much has been achieved in a short time. Wild excesses of fascistic zeal have been avoided, yet the great Australian apathy has been in some measure stirred. All the indications are that these issues will demand serious, concerted action for a long while to come.

At the time of writing, changes in public morality have been occurring with great rapidity for three or four years. Significant changes in the law have occurred, and changes in public opinion on numerous moral issues indicate that pressures for further changes will come over the next few years. To rush headlong into these in response to pressure-groups, who present opinion as if it were fact, would be dangerous. If standards are to be maintained or raised, it will be necessary to spell out where lies the basis for standards, and why the abandoning of such standards will ultimately prove disastrous. The present strength of public support is such that the Festival of Light and these other groups can play a major role in presenting evidence at all levels. However, there is no time to waste.

14

Is There Anything I Can Do?

The world expects of Christians that they will raise their voices so loudly and clearly and so formulate their protest that not even the simplest man can have the slightest doubt about what they are saying. . . We stand in need of folk who have determined to speak directly and unmistakably and, come what may, to stand by what they have said.

Albert Camus

Many in the community are aware of changes in our society which appear undesirable. It is not always easy to know what to do. Most people dislike making themselves conspicuous over some issue or other; many feel that, even if they could do something, it would be of no use; and there is always the problem of appearing "different" or of experiencing ridicule for seeking to counter what appears to be popular opinion. Yet the essence of a democratic way of life is that all should play their part, that even minority opinion is entitled to a hearing, and that the electorate should be informed and active. Anything less results in unrepresentative government. Apathy can lead only to deservedly poor standards.

When it comes to the control of material being disseminated through the mass media, we must ask, "Whose standards are being applied?" It has been indicated above that it is dangerous if those standards are set by those who control the popular media of press, radio, and TV. Those who believe that censorship should be abolished should be, and in some cases are, active to further their beliefs. At the same time, those who firmly believe that our standards are being seriously eroded have a duty firmly to express their concern. The practice of censorship is entirely consistent with democratic principles when managed responsibly.

Action to maintain or regain standards is undoubtedly called for if we are to prevent significant harm to individuals and to society. It was the view of an American judge that "over a long period of time the indiscriminate dissemination of materials, the essential character of which is to degrade sex, will have an eroding influence on moral standards."[1] Even those who are quick to object to the control of sexual material will often point to the hazards inherent in the trivializing of human values and in the disregard for human dignity which characterizes so much contemporary entertainment.

The first imperative for action is to seek to make a **positive** rather than a **negative** impact. It is too easy to say, "I don't like that", or, "It offends me". The Minister, and others responsible for decisions, need to know what is wanted, if productive changes are to be brought about. One may view a film and find it unacceptable for public viewing; but it is necessary to be able to say **why**, if one's opinion is to carry weight with others.

Sometimes, however, a stand against unacceptable material must be resolutely taken, even if accusations of being "negative", or "wowserish", or "paternalistic" are levelled. As was indicated above, effective quality control will be possible only as the reject is identified and thrown out, allowing the good standard material to circulate.

AVENUES FOR ACTION

The kind of action that may be taken will vary. Sometimes a person may act individually to great effect; more often it is necessary to work collectively, either through existing organizations or by forming new ones. Those with particular skills may have a special responsiblity to act or speak in ways not open to others, but every citizen should accept his right and responsibility to play some part.

Individuals now have a range of possibilities open to them:

(a) Before acting, it is important to be informed. The fact that the basis for Federal decisions on censorship is made public is commendable; it is possible to know what is being attempted at a Federal level in this area. The thoughtful citizen should also become familiar with State policies. He should take an active interest in the way mass media present information, critically evaluating whether there are unwarranted biases.

(b) Parents, especially those with young children, need to keep a constant watch on what is made available to their children. The TV should not be considered a baby-sitter, nor should it claim the time and attention which parents could use better in other ways. Wise parents will watch selected TV programs **with** their children and discuss the experience. The pressures of advertising will also deserve thoughtful discussion. Criteria governing TV advertising directed to children are to be found in Appendix 2.

The last few years have seen a healthy upsurge of interest in the impact of TV on viewers in Australia, and the consequent establishment of groups dedicated to working for better standards. On a national level, the Advisory Committee on Children's TV Programs, under the auspices of the Australian Broadcasting Control Board, publishes helpful material and invites active response from parents.

LET YOUR VOICE BE HEARD

(c) Expressions of approval and disapproval should be registered. A letter to the paper, a phone call to the TV studio, a comment over radio talk-back can contribute to the development of a balanced program of entertainment. Words of praise for what is good are too infrequently given.

When material over radio or TV proves unacceptable, several lines of communication are open. Contact with the station manager is sometimes worthwhile, provided a well-reasoned point is made, but those who protest can usually expect a hostile reply at this level. A letter to the Australian Broadcasting Control Board will receive serious and reasoned attention. It is a wise move when writing to the Board about a TV program to send a carbon-copy for information to the station manager (or vice versa). Not only is this a courteous thing to do, but it also ensures that each knows that the other knows what has been written, and the response will be influenced by this knowledge. With commercial stations, contact with sponsors can also prove effective. Advertisers wish to please potential customers and will not sponsor a program which generates an adverse reaction.

Among the more subtly-intrusive influences to be watched carefully is the review of new films contained in the daily press. Carried through with an air of sophistication, many a review of a thoroughly unacceptable film can be presented as if it were an enriching experience. Clear thinking will be necessary to discern the deceptive phrases, and a letter of protest should help to reduce this tendency to promote the obscene as if it were art.

(d) An approach to those responsible for government is considered too infrequently. The local council member and members of State or Federal parliaments take office in order to serve those who elect them. These people are charged with the responsibility of representing their voters. The individual who is uncertain whether action is required can quite properly contact his local members and discuss it. Most elected representatives welcome such contact and will respond positively. It does not, of course, follow that the individual's wishes will always be fulfilled; but involvement in community affairs by the greatest possible number is desirable so that all shades of opinion can be heard.

(e) Each person can also encourage others to be active. One often hears a friend or neighbour say, "What a shocking show!", or, "How offensive that advertisement was!"; yet, if one asks, "What have you done about it?", it is rare to find that anything has been attempted. It is important to act, and to encourage others to discover that action can bring results.

SUPPORT COLLECTIVE ACTION

Collective action can prove constructive where the individual cannot act alone:

(a) The basis for most of the significant decisions in a community is political action. Active involvement with a local political group is, therefore, one way of making a contribution. Many of Christian conviction have reservations about political involvement, but it is doubtful whether this position can be justified. There is a real need for men and women with clearly-thought-out convictions to be active within the political arena at all levels. Those Christians who have already taken this step and entered politics, currently bear a heavy responsibility, as so much legislation has moral overtones. They deserve a great deal of support, encouragement, and advice from Christians in the electorates which they represent.

(b) For some purposes, a pressure-group can be set up for the specific purpose of drawing together the resources of those who wish to make a point. Reference has been made in the previous chapter to the various groups which have been formed to take action in specific arenas.

Whereas Christians have tended to shun political action along party lines, there has been strong support given to such pressure-groups. This is good — much better than Christians seeking to set up a separate Christian political party. Triton offers good advice when he says, "We believe that Christians should act to improve the laws and customs and structures of society as they are able to do so by appropriate means. To fail to do so is to opt out of our God-given responsibilities as citizens. We believe also that since political action requires, at least in a democracy, action by groups of people who are of one mind, however unofficial these groups may be, we cannot escape the responsibility of trying to organize expressions of opinion, persuade others by rational means to agree with us and vote with us, and to develop a coherent Christian view on questions where specifically moral or theological issues are at stake." [2]

(c) Particular issues can justify the use of petitions to parliament. This procedure is a recognized feature of the democratic process. With careful presentation, and preferably with the assistance of mass media coverage to publicize the issue at stake, communities in Australia are of such a size that petition-signing can represent an informed response and not just a meaningless reaction. This process can also go some way toward showing parliamentarians where the strength of opinion lies. However, petitions should be used sparingly; this avenue is in danger of being overworked. They must not be made a substitute for thoughtful, individual action.

SERVICE GROUPS CAN HELP

(d) Various community organizations which exist for broadly humanitarian purposes, as well as service organizations (like Rotary, Apex, Lions), should be encouraged to ally themselves with efforts to preserve high standards in the community. Where the status or dignity of womanhood appears to be threatened, it is right to call upon women's organizations to support all efforts to counter such influences. Indeed, unless the age of chivalry is gone for ever, men's organizations could also be actively involved. Increasingly the needs of children are being disregarded or manipulated. These same groups, together with such bodies as parent-teacher associations and school councils, need to exercise at least a watching brief.

Prevention is in many ways better than cure. As voluntary and State welfare agencies stagger beneath the load of need which accumulates from problems like alcoholism, divorce, crime, delinquency, and attempted suicide, it seems reasonable to expect support from such agencies also in efforts to provide a climate of thought which will counter socially-destructive forces. Just as long as we continue to accept the trivial, the vicious, and the distorted as the customary components of our entertainment media, we may expect our social pathology problems to continue to increase. As long as hedonism is portrayed as a virtue, irresponsibility is praised, and promiscuity actively condoned, we can scarcely expect to gain control of problems like alcoholism, drug-taking, or unwanted pregnancies.

BE UP AND DOING

It may be that a long-standing failure to act, due to uncertainty or complacency, has resulted in the present situation where many undesirable changes are occurring with few to challenge them.

It has proved necessary to defend good standards by public protest, because long-established principles have been disregarded. But increased awareness and support will make it possible to move to a more constructive position. Guidelines can and should be given; positive advice should be made available to Parliament; high standards should be represented to the mass media. Whose standards shall they be?

Let the reader consider, and respond as he sees fit. To Edmund Burke is attributed the aphorism, "All that is needed for evil to triumph is that good men do nothing".

References

Chapter 1

1. V.B. Cline, *Where Do You Draw the Line?* (Utah: Brigham Young University Press, 1974).

Chapter 2

1. H.M. Hyde, *A History of Pornography* (New York: Farrar Straus & Giroux, 1965).
2. A.P. Klausler, *Censorship, Obscenity, and Sex* (St. Louis: Concordia Publishing House, 1967).
3. A.P. Klausler, *op. cit.*
4. Judge H. Windeyer, Crowe v Graham and Others. In *Australian Law Journal Review*, 41, 1967/68.
5. Hans Mol, Family and Religion. In *The Family in Australia*, eds. J. Krupinski and A. Stoller (Sydney: Pergamon Press, 1974).
6. J.S. Gummer, *The Permissive Society* (London: Cassell, 1971).
7. Francis Grim, *Attempted Rape of South Africa* (South Africa: Heart Publishers, 1974).
8. *The Australian* (Sydney: January 25, 1974).
9. E. Dearn, *Pornography Degrades* (Sydney: Renda Publications, 1975).

Chapter 4

1. J.H. Court, Censorship — A Conservative View. In *Conservatism as Heresy*, ed. J.J. Ray (Sydney: A.N.Z. Book Co., 1974).
2. J. Dobson, *Dare to Discipline* (London: Coverdale House Publishers, 1971).
3. See, e.g., S. Swerling, Who's getting at our kids? (Mimeographed, 1973).
4. Mary Whitehouse, *Who Does She Think She Is?* (London: New English Library, 1972).
5. A. Walker, quoted by J.D. Traill.
6. J.D. Traill, Humanism and the campaign for "reform" of social laws. In *Why Abortion?* Proceedings of a public meeting in Melbourne, June 1, 1971 (Human Life Research Foundation).
7. O. Guinness, *The Dust of Death* (London: IVP, 1973).
8. This section is based on a paper first published in the *Lutheran Theological Journal* (Adelaide: 6, 1972) pp. 95-104.
9. *Empire Times*, Flinders University student newspaper (Adelaide: October, 1971).
10. Quoted in Mary Whitehouse, *op. cit.*
11. James Michener, *Kent State — What Happened and Why?* (London: Secker and Warburg, 1972).
12. R. Neville, *Play Power* (Harmondsworth: Penguin, 1972).
13. United Nations, Office of Public Information, 1948.
14. UNICEF Declaration, 1959.
15. Editorial, *Women* (1970, *2*, 2), pp. 1 and 64.
16. E.G. Gibson, The Future of Australia: national and spiritual. Lecture, Victor Harbor, South Australia, January, 1974.

Chapter 5

1. *The Advertiser* (Adelaide: March, 1972).
2. M.A. Hill and W.C. Link, *Report of the Commission on Obscenity and Pornography* (New York: Bantam Books, 1970).
3. V. Packard, *The Sexual Wilderness* (New York: Pocket Books, 1970).
4. A. Huxley, *Ends and Means* (London: Chatto and Windus, 1965).
5. V.A Demant, *An Exposition of Christian Sex Ethics* (London: Hodder, 1963).

6. P.A. Sorokin, *The Sociology of Revolution* (New York: Fertig, 1967).
7. P.A. Sorokin, *The American Sex Revolution* (Boston: Porter Sargent, 1957).
8. P.J. Allen, ed., *Pitrim A. Sorokin in Review* (The American Sociological Forum, Durham N.C.: Duke University Press, 1963).
9. B. Kutschinsky, *The Effect of Pornography on Sex Crimes in Denmark* (Copenhagen: New Social Science Monographs, 1970).
10. *The Observer* (London: January 26, 1971).
11. Mary Whitehouse, *Who Does She Think She Is?* (London: New English Library, 1972).
12. J.S. Gummer, *The Permissive Society* (London: Cassell, 1971).
13. R. Ben-Veniste, Pornography and Sex Crime: The Danish Experience. In *Technical Reports of the Commission on Obscenity and Pornography*, Vol. 7 (Washington, D.C.: U.S. Government Printing Office, 1971) pp. 245-261.
14. J.S. Gummer, *op. cit.*
15. *The Daily Telegraph* (London: January 16, 1974).
16. Quoted in *Pornography: The Longford Report* (London: Coronet Books, 1972) p. 126.
17. C.B. Reifler, *et al.* Pornography: An experimental study of effects. In *American Journal of Psychiatry* (1971, *128*, 5) pp. 575-582.
18. G. Schmidt and V. Sigusch, Sex differences in responses to psychosexual stimulation by film and slides. In *Journal of Sex Research* (1970, *6*, 4) pp. 268-283.
19. B. Kutschinsky, Pornography in Denmark. In *Studies in Pornography* (Copenhagen: New Social Science Monographs, 1970).
20. L.R. Shilton, ed., *No, No, Calcutta* (Adelaide: Brolga Books, 1971).
21. J. Facius, *The Little White Book* (Melbourne: S. John Bacon, 1972).
22. James M. Wall, *Church and Cinema* (Grand Rapids: Eerdmans, 1971).
23. R.G. Green and L.J. Berkowitz, Some conditions facilitating the occurrence of aggression after the observation of violence. In *Journal of Personality* (1966, 35) p. 666.
24. J.A. Cheyne and R.H. Walters, Punishment and Prohibition: Some Origins of Self-Control. In *New Directions in Psychology*, 4, ed. R. Newcombe (New York: Holt, Rinehart and Winston, 1970).
25. D. Maddison, in a personal letter to the author, 1972.
26. R.M. Liebert, J.M. Neale, and E.S. Davidson, *The Early Window* (New York: Pergamon, 1973).
27. H.J. Eysenck, *Psychology is about People* (Harmondsworth: Allen Lane, 1972).

Chapter 6

1. D. Williams, *Trousered Apes* (London: Churchill Press, 1971).
2. R. Gauer, in *The National Decency Reporter* (1972, *9*, 2).
3. H. Caterer in *The Sunday Mail* (Adelaide: April 29, 1972).
4. F. Schaeffer, *Escape from Reason* (London: IVP Pocketbooks, 1968).
5. Max Harris, *The Australian* (Sydney: May 6, 1972).
6. J.S. Gummer, *The Permissive Society* (London: Cassell, 1971).
7. D. Maddison, Mental Health in the Permissive Society. In *Medical Journal of Australia* (1971, *58*, 1, 17) pp. 908-914.
8. W. Hall, *London Evening News* (London: August 29, 1972).
9. K.E. Davis and G.N. Braucht, Exposure to Pornography, Character and Sexual Deviance: A Retrospective Survey. In *Technical Reports of the Commission on Obscenity and Pornography*, Vol. 7 (Washington, D.C.: U.S. Government Printing Office, 1971) pp. 173-244.
10. V.B. Cline, *Where Do You Draw the Line?* (Utah: Brigham Young University Press, 1974).

Chapter 7

* This chapter is based on a paper read to the Human Life Research Foundation in Melbourne, October, 1973, and contained in *Pornography and Human Sexuality*, ed. J.A. Santamaria (Melbourne: Beckett Press, 1974).

1. E. Kronhausen and P. Kronhausen, The Psychology of Pornography. In *The Encyclopaedia of Sexual Behaviour*, eds. A. Ellis and A. Abarbanel (New York: Hawthorn Books, 1967).
2. G. Schmidt and V. Sigusch, Sex differences in response to psychosexual stimulation by films and slides. In *Journal of Sex Research* (1970, *6*, 4) pp. 268-283.
3. D.M. Amoroso, M. Brown, M. Pruesse, E.E. Ware, and D.W. Pilkey, The effects of physiological measurement and presence of others in ratings of erotic stimuli. In *Canadian Journal of Behavioural Science* (1972, *4*, 3) pp. 191-203.
4. C.B. Reifler, J. Howard, M.A. Lipton, M.B. Liptzin, and D.E. Widman, Pornography: An experimental study of effects. In *American Journal of Psychiatry* (1971, *128*, 5) pp. 573-582.
5. H. Nawy, The San Francisco Erotic Marketplace. In *Technical Reports of the Commission on Obscenity and Pornography*, Vol. 4 (Washington, D.C.: U.S. Government Printing Office, 1971) pp. 155-224.
6. D. Holbrook, *The Masks of Hate* (London: Pergamon, 1972).
7. D. Holbrook, *Pornography and Hate* (London: The Responsible Society, 1972).
8. B. Clunies-Ross, *The Bulletin* (Sydney: June 27, 1970).
9. D. Holbrook, *Sex and Dehumanization* (London: Pitman, 1972).
10. J.H. Court, *Stand Up and Be Counted* (Adelaide: Lutheran Publishing House, 1973).
11. R. Stoller, Pornography and Perversion. In *Archives of General Psychiatry* (1970, *22*, 490), reprinted in *The Case against Pornography*, ed. D. Holbrook (London: Tom Stacey, 1972).
12. Editorial, *The Times* (London: September 3, 1970).
13. H. Cox, *The Secular City* (London: SCM Press, 1965).
14. R. May, *Love and Will* (New York: W.W. Norton and Co., 1969).
15. D. Holbrook, *The Case Against Pornography* (London: Tom Stacey, 1972).
16. Lord Longford, *Pornography: The Longford Report* (London: Coronet Books, 1972).
17. L.R. Shilton, ed., *No, No, Calcutta* (Adelaide: Brolga Books, 1971).
18. M.A. Hill and W.C. Link, *Report of the Commission on Obscenity and Pornography* (New York: Bantam Books, 1970).
19. H.J. Eysenck, *Psychology is about People* (Harmondsworth: Allen Lane, 1972).
20. J.H. Court, Pornography — Personal and Societal Effects. In *Liberation Movements and Psychiatry*, ed. N. McConaghy. Geigy Psychiatric Symposium 1973. Vol. 2 Ciba-Geigy, 1974.
21. M.J. Goldstein, H.S. Kant, L.L. Judd, C.J. Rice, and R. Green, Exposure to pornography and sexual behaviour in deviant and normal groups. In *Technical Reports of the Commission on Obscenity and Pornography*, Vol. 7 (Washington, D.C.: U.S. Government Printing Office, 1971) pp. 1-90.
22. Schmidt and Sigusch, *op. cit.*
23. C.E. Walker, Erotic stimuli and the aggressive sexual offender. In *Technical Reports of the Commission on Obscenity and Pornography*, Vol. 7 (Washington, D.C.: U.S. Government Printing Office, 1971) pp. 91-148.

24. J.H. Court, *op. cit.*
25. J. Selosse, Statistical report on violent crime in Austria, England and Wales, France, Italy, and Sweden (1960-70). 10th Conference of Directors of Criminological Research Institutes, Strasbourg (Brussels: Council of Europe, 1972).
26. H. Nawy, The San Francisco Erotic Marketplace. In *Technical Reports of the Commission on Obscenity and Pornography*, Vol. 4 (Washington, D.C.: U.S. Government Printing Office, 1970) pp. 155-244.
27. K. Whitehorn, Rape: fact and fantasy. In *The Bulletin* (Sydney: August 31, 1974).
28. S. Feshbach, The drive-reducing function of fantasy behaviour. In *Journal of Abnormal and Social Psychology* (1955, *50*, 1) pp. 3-12.
29. R.M. Liebert, J.M. Neale, and E.S. Davidson, *The Early Window* (New York: Pergamon, 1972).
30. G. Steiner, The Freakish Passion. In *Psychology Today* (1973, *6*, 9) p. 62.
31. B. Kutchinsky, Towards an explanation of the decrease in registered sex crimes in Copenhagen (Copenhagen: New Social Science Monographs, 1970) pp. 99-159.
32. D. Holbrook, *Sex and Dehumanization* (London: Pitman, 1972).
33. R. Neville, quoted in *Pornography: The Longford Report* (London: Coronet Books, 1972).
34. H.J. Eysenck, *op. cit.*

Chapter 8

1. A. Bandura, *Principles of Behaviour Modification* (New York: Holt, Rinehart, and Winston, 1969).
2. M.A. Jeeves, Science — A Contemporary God? In *Interchange* (1972, 11) pp. 179-190.
3. Sir Michael Swann, Speech to Royal TV Society Convention, Cambridge, September, 1973.
4. J. Randall, Arthur Bremer and Mental Health. In *American Psychologists Association Monitor* (Washington: 1972, *3*, 7) p. 3.
5. L.R. Shilton, ed., *No, No, Calcutta* (Adelaide: Brolga Books, 1971).
6. K. Heller and G.A. Marlatt, Verbal conditioning, behaviour therapy and behaviour change. In *Behaviour Therapy: Appraisal and Status*, ed. C.M. Franks (New York: McGraw Hill, 1969).
7. M.A. Hill and W.C. Link, *Report of the Commission on Obscenity and Pornography* (New York: Bantam Books, 1970).
8. H.J. Eysenck, *Smoking, Health and Personality* (London: Four Square Books, 1965).
9. R.G. Farmer, Censorship and Sex Education in the Home. Symposium on Censorship and Psychology, Canberra, 1972.
10. L. Berkowitz and J. Macaulay, The Contagion of Criminal Violence. In *Sociometry* (1971, *34*, 2) pp. 238-260.

Chapter 9

1,2,3. See Recommended Reading, page 118.
4. R. Brine, quoted in *Time* (New York: April 5, 1971).
5. J. Haynes, Problems of Censorship. In *Interchange* (1970, *2*, 4).
6. Poll on Social Issues, in *The Age* (Melbourne: July 30, 1973).
7. D. Holbrook, in *The Sunday Telegraph* (London: December 23, 1973).
8. J. Randall, Arthur Bremer and Mental Health. In *American Psychologists Association Monitor* (Washington: 1972, *3*, 7) p. 3.
9. *The News* (San Antonio, Texas: November 14, 1973).
10. W. Barclay, *Ethics in a Permissive Society* (London: Fontana, 1971).
11. Mary Whitehouse, *Who Does She Think She Is?* (London: New English Library, 1972).
12. *The Advocate* (Melbourne: January 17, 1974).

13. H.R. Rookmaaker, *Modern Art and the Death of a Culture* (London: IVP, 1970).

Chapter 10

1. *Television and Religion* (London: University of London Press, 1964) p. 41.
2. Hans Mol, *Religion in Australia*, Ch. 8 (Melbourne: Nelson, 1971).
3. *Philippians 4.8.*
4. A.N. Triton, *Whose World?* (London: IVP Pocketbooks, 1970).
5. J. Stone, Letter to *The Australian* (Sydney: May, 1971).

Chapter 11

1. *The Sunday Mail* (Adelaide: February 1, 1974).
2. D. Maddison, Mental Health in the Permissive Society. In *Medical Journal of Australia* (1971, *58*, 1, 17) pp. 908-914.

Chapter 12

1. W. Barclay, *Ethics in a Permissive Society* (London: Fontana, 1971).
2. A. Nichols, *The Communicators* (Sydney: Pilgrim Productions, 1972).
3. D. Maddison, Mental Health in the Permissive Society. In *Medical Journal of Australia* (1971, *58*, 1, 17) pp. 908-914.
4. B. Spock, *Decent and Indecent* (Harmondsworth: Penguin, 1972).
5. E. Campbell and H. Whitmore, *Freedom in Australia* (Sydney: Sydney University Press, 1973).
6. *The Advertiser* (Adelaide: December, 1971).
7. *Time* (New York: February 11, 1974).
8. W. Barclay, *op. cit.*
9. H.J. Eysenck, *Psychology is About People* (Harmondsworth: Allen Lane, 1972).
10. D.J. Lawrence, *Pornography and Obscenity* (1929). Quoted by A. Beal, *Selected Literary Criticism* (London: Heinemann, 1967).
11. L. Berkowitz and J. Macaulay, The Contagion of Criminal Violence. In *Sociometry* (1971, *34*, 2) p. 240.
12. K. Fleming, Dr. Spock, Slightly Revised. In *Human Behaviour* (1974, 3, 8) pp. 25-29.
13. R. Huntford, *The New Totalitarians* (Harmondsworth: Allen Lane, 1973).

Chapter 13

1. D.O. Moberg, *The Great Reversal* (London: Scripture Union, 1973).
2. J. Campbell, Democracy faces the crunch. In *The Advertiser* (Adelaide: June 8, 1974).
3. L.R. Shilton, ed., *No, No, Calcutta* (Adelaide: Brolga Books, 1971).
4. J.H. Court, Pornography, Violence and Hate. Address to Melbourne Festival of Light Rally, April, 1974.
5. Mary Whitehouse, *Who Does She Think She Is?* (London: New English Library, 1971).
6. B. Faust, *The Australian Humanist* (1973, *28*) pp. 4-7.
7. J.H. Court, Boning up on the Subject. In *The Australian Humanist* (1974, *29*) pp. 5-8.
8. J.H. Court and H. Caterer, *Stand Up and Be Counted* (Adelaide: Lutheran Publishing House, 1973).
9. D. Hilliard and J. Warhurst, Festival of Light. In *Current Affairs Bulletin* (Sydney: 1974, *50*, 9) pp. 13-19.

Chapter 14

1. Sex and Morals 1954-63. In *The Criminal Law Review*, April, 1964. See J.N.D. Anderson, *Morality, Law and Grace* (London: Tyndale Press, 1972).
2. A.N. Triton, *Whose World?* (London: IVP Pocketbooks, 1970).

Recommended Reading

J.N.D. Anderson, *Morality, Law and Grace* (London: Tyndale Press, 1972). (A professor of law looks at the relationship between crime and sin, and the involvement of the law in morality.)

W. Barclay, *Ethics in a Permissive Society* (London: Fontana, 1971). (Originally the Baird Lectures presented on TV, this book discusses a wide variety of ethical issues from a Christian viewpoint.)

V.B. Cline, *Where do You draw the Line?* (Utah: Brigham Young University Press, 1974).
(A psychologist draws together evidence on the effects of pornography and violence.)

J.S. Gummer, *The Permissive Society* (London: Cassell, 1971).

A.P. Klausler, *Censorship, Obscenity, and Sex* (St. Louis: Concordia, 1967). (A documentation of the background to legislation in the United States relating to censorship and obscenity, with coverage of community response.)

Lord Longford, *Pornography: The Longford Report* (London: Coronet Books, 1972).

B. Mitchell, *Law, Morality, and Religion in a Secular Society* (London: Oxford University Press, 1967).

D.O. Moberg, *The Great Reversal* (London: Scripture Union, 1973).

H.R. Rookmaaker, *Modern Art and the Death of a Culture* (London: IVP, 1970).
(The history of art is taken as the basis for discussing the cultural values being expressed. The contemporary note of despair is matched by recommendations for a positive response.)

L. Shilton, ed., *No, No, Calcutta* (Adelaide: Brolga Books, 1971).
(A book which not only traces the historic legal action taken against "Oh! Calcutta!", but also discusses the general issues of censorship and pornography.)

A.N. Triton, *Whose World?* (London: IVP, 1970).
(A treatment of the Christian's attitude to the material world, culture, politics, technology, and society.)

Mary Whitehouse, *Who Does She Think She Is?* (London: New English Library, 1972).
(An autobiographical account of the struggle to preserve standards in Britain.)

Appendix 1

[A statement concerning the patrons of sex shops, which was circulated by the Community Standards Organization to members of Australian State and Federal Parliaments, to assist in the formation of informed judgements about the patrons of such shops. It includes information more generally relevant to the availability of printed pornography, irrespective of its place of sale.]

SEX SHOPS – FOR WHOM DO THEY CATER?

In South Australia it is too soon to know who will be the regular patrons of sex shops. For now we may suppose that curiosity about a novelty will attract many casual onlookers, of whom only a few will buy. However, the intention of the owners is clearly to remain in business. Will that business be for a select few? Will it benefit those who attend? Will there be any repercussions for the community at large?

In the absence of much knowledge it would be easy to speculate. Rather than do that, the reports from elsewhere can give us a clue. A study was made in the Los Angeles area of those who attend sex shops, and the following includes a summary of what was found out about these patrons.

The whole study concerned the reactions of various sexually-deviate groups to erotica, but included a group of 52 patrons of "adult bookstores" who responded to a request for information. A control group of normals was also interviewed. We do not know how representative these 52 are; simply, that they are "a sample of people who do acknowledge frequent contact and use of these materials in their sex lives". Nor do we know how representative were the control group, since of 133 people contacted, 63 agreed to participate.

And since the procedure was based on asking questions about past experiences, we do not know how much bias, poor memory, or repression has affected results. Dr. Michael Goldstein and his colleagues, in reporting their work, recognize these problems, but present the findings for consideration.

They call their subjects "users" of erotica. Asked to say how often they had seen various kinds of erotica in adolescence they found that "people who are currently avid buyers and consumers of commercial pornography indicate a pattern similar to the sex deviate sample". This meant that they had less often seen portrayals of sexual activity than normals. Asked about recent experience of erotica, a reverse pattern appeared (a finding also noted with homosexuals) — that is, a low reported contact with erotica by users in adolescence becomes a high contact, and this "suggests some sort of compensatory interest pattern".

They were asked in various ways what effect erotica had for them. 78% reported that they responded with masturbation afterwards (compared with 37% of controls). The use of the material during masturbation was 40% for users (11% of controls). In 56% of cases, users reported being excited to sexual relations (compared with 48% of controls).

Asked if they would wish to try out the particular sexual act they had seen portrayed, 30% of normal controls said yes, and 58% of users said yes. Asked if they did actually imitate, 22% of the users said yes (13% of controls).

Some of the interview was devoted to exploring the background these users came from. Goldstein says:

> "They report significantly more permissive parental attitudes toward childhood nudity than controls. As teenagers, there appeared to be a shift towards less nudity tolerance. They report a high parental awareness of their interest in erotic materials and little parental concern or punishment in discovering this. They report great comfort in talking about sex and a very tolerant view of homosexuality, although they report a low incidence of this activity for themselves. They advocate very liberal sex attitudes with over 75% approving of pre-marital sex for all persons. They report a later age of first intercourse than most other groups and a considerable number had their first experience with a prostitute. They contain a substantial number who have had more than seven (7) extra-marital affairs. Their frequency of sexual behaviour is close to that reported by controls. They report achieving orgasm through a wider variety of means than controls (light petting, oral stimulation, and oral-genital stimulation) and report high enjoyment in sexual relations."

Goldstein's studies were confined almost exclusively to males, as "we hypothesized that exposure and impact would be greatest in that group". One can endorse the relative degree of exposure but question whether impact is greatest in the male. Measures of sexual arousal certainly confirm this, but other reactions in females would be worth knowing about. This also raises a question of who the users really are. In actual fact, this group are better described as purchasers. It has been shown by other studies that females also see much of this material.

Several other more superficial studies were carried out and reported to the American Presidential Commission on Obscenity and Pornography. These involved observing patrons of adult bookstores and assessing (chiefly from observation) who came. Studies are uniform in agreeing that more than 90% are men, predominantly middle-class and middle-aged. They come to the shops alone. Probably the majority are married. These characteristics held good for several cities across America, as well as in Copenhagen. About 20-30% of patrons actually buy anything.

That the material does not remain with those who buy it, is evident from a study by Abelson (reported to the Commission).

> "Few people report they buy erotic materials. Only 5% of the men who have seen non-movie visual depictions in the past two years report having bought the most recent depiction they have seen; an additional 8% report having seen it at a newsstand or bookstore; but 53% report having been shown the depiction or given it by someone else. A larger proportion of men report having bought the most recent textual depictions they have read (26%). Only 4% read it at a bookstore or newsstand; 64% report having obtained it from someone else at no cost. The figures for women are roughly comparable."

In this connection, Keating makes a useful summary of reports presented to the American Commission which relate to surveys of sex-shop and sex-film patrons.

He says:

"The Commission Report suggests that the primary purchasers of erotica appear to be well-educated, middle-class, males in their 30s and 40s. It should be noted that this is based on studies nearly all in downtown urban areas where a surveyor 'guessed' at the age, socio-economic level, etc., of those he saw in 'adult book-stores' and movies. Where interviews were conducted, they consisted of approaching men as they emerged from an 'adult movie' and having an 'informal conversation over coffee' with them (no notes were taken until later). And of 270 people approached in the Winick study, only 100 agreed to 'have coffee', creating sampling problems. When they tried to get people to fill out questionnaires (as in the Nawy study of the 'San Francisco Marketplace') only 29 out of 150 bookshop customers co-operated, and 190 out of 800 movie patrons so obliged. This makes generalizing about these data extremely risky. Massey (1970) in his analysis of the Denver area concluded that the type of customer is related to the **location of the store and time of day.**"

Probably the major issue is who *consumes* and *uses* pornography, not so much who *buys* it. Because for every purchaser of hard-core materials there may be 10-100 viewers or users of the merchandise. In the Abelson National Survey of Youth and Adults we find that girls 15 to 20 see most pornography (for females), and young men in the age range of 15 to 29 get the heaviest doses. Abelson found that more boys than adult men have seen visual pornography (87% v 80%) and more girls have seen this than adult females (80% v 53%). This means in sum that the heavy users and most highly exposed people to pornography are adolescent females (among women) and adolescent and young adult males (among men).

Though his samples are not random, in Nawy's study of the "San Francisco Marketplace", 70% of the patrons of erotica he surveyed attend sex movies once a month or more. He also found that 49% of these people were currently having sex with two or more partners in and out of their households, and 25% had been having sex with 6 or more partners in the past year. Frequency of intercourse rates were very high for his sample, suggesting that erotica may have a "booster" or "accelerating" effect on sex activity. In any event, the data outside the laboratory, where people are studied in their own environment, suggest that those interested in erotica or pornography consume it regularly and for "sexual" reasons. But this is suggestive only because of flawed sampling.

Summary Comment

Sex shops in other countries appear to cater for a limited group of people — male, middle-aged, middle-class, often married. In some ways they show greater similarity to sexual deviates than they do to others not frequenting such shops. They commonly had less-than-average exposure to sexual materials when young. On obtaining it later, they use it as an aid to fantasy and to enacting immature psychosexuality. They very often wish to engage in the sexual acts they see depicted, and some actually do. Most of them are in favour of pre-marital sex for everybody, and have a large number of sexual partners themselves. They do not keep their purchases to themselves, since in the area of pictures and texts, most encounters are with material that has been passed on. Among women this is most apparent for the 15-20 age group.

Sources

M.J. Goldstein, Exposure to Erotic Stimuli and Sexual Deviance. Paper presented to American Psychologists Association Conference, Miami Beach, September 1970.

M.J. Goldstein, H.S. Kant, L.L. Judd, C.J. Rice, and R. Green, Experience with Pornography: Rapists, Pedophiles, Homosexuals, Transsexuals, and Controls. In *Sexual Behaviour* (1971, *1*, 1) pp.1-15.

H.S. Kant and M.J. Goldstein, *Pornography, Psychology Today* (December 1970).

M.A. Hill and W.C. Link, *Report on the Commission on Obscenity and Pornography* (New York: Bantam Books, 1970).

Appendix 2

SOME EXISTING FEDERAL STANDARDS

While it may appear that standards have changed, in fact, it is the *thorough interpretation* of those standards which has been allowed to lapse. If standards are to be maintained, it is necessary to be informed what existing standards are recognized. It then remains for the informed citizen to ensure that the democratic process actually operates and is not allowed to fall into disrepair.

The following standards are those which apply throughout Australia. Legislation in the individual Australian States varies, and is too diverse to justify inclusion here.

1. Books

Censorship is maintained through the Customs Act 1901-1968 and associated regulations. Section 50 of this Act gives the Governor-General power to prohibit the importation of goods into Australia, and the prohibition may be absolute or conditional.

The Customs (Prohibited Imports) Regulations include r.4A(1) which states:

> "This regulation applies to goods that, whether of their own nature or having regard to any literary or other work or matter that is embodied, recorded or reproduced in, or can be reproduced from, the goods —
>
> (a) are blasphemous, indecent or obscene; or
>
> (b) unduly emphasise matters of sex, horror, violence, or crime, or are likely to encourage depravity, and to advertising matter relating to such goods."

Regulation 4A(2) states that importation of such goods is prohibited unless, after he has obtained a report from the chairman or acting chairman of the National Literature Board of Review or from the

Registrar-General of Health, the Minister grants permission to import.

A full discussion of these regulations and their application may be found in "Freedom in Australia".[1]

2. Films

The Customs Act 1901-1968 is again the basis for censorship, with the Customs (Cinematograph Films) Regulations providing the criteria. r.13 states:

"(1) Subject to the next succeeding sub-regulation, a film shall not be passed under this Part if, in the opinion of the Board —

(a) the film or advertising matter is blasphemous, indecent, or obscene;

(b) the film or advertising matter is likely to be injurious to morality, or to encourage or incite to crime;

(c) the film or advertising matter is likely to be offensive to the people of a friendly nation or to the people of a part of the Queen's dominions; or

(d) the film or advertising matter depicts any matter the exhibition of which is undesirable in the public interest."

Discussion on how the machinery actually operates may be found in "Freedom in Australia".[2]

3. Television

The Australian Broadcasting Control Board operates within the terms of reference provided by the Broadcasting and Television Act 1942-1969. This Board has drawn up recommendations which are not legally enforceable but represent guidelines for the commercial stations to follow. The ABC has also indicated its acceptance of these standards, which will be followed in the presentation of programs.

The Board's guide, entitled "Television Programme Standards", says, by way of introduction, that "responsibility for what is viewed in the home must to some extent lie with the viewer, but it is reasonable for him to expect that all programs will be acceptable in terms of social standards current in the Australian community and that, consistent with the principle stated in the Act, they should be in the best interests of the general public".

Standards are given for general, family, and children's viewing. They include:

General Program Standards

(5) Fundamentally these Standards require the observance in programs of good taste and common sense. In general, this calls for respect for the law and for the rights and sensitivities of the public, and regard for the special needs of children.

(6) The basic requirements which must always be observed in the presentation of television programs are that:

(a) No program may contain any matter which is —

(i) contrary to law;

(ii) blasphemous, indecent, or obscene;

(iii) likely to encourage crime;

(iv) likely to be injurious to community well-being or morality; or

(v) otherwise undesirable in the public interest.

(b) Programs which contain matter that is not generally suitable for viewing by children must not be televised at times when large numbers of children are likely to have access to television receivers.

Family Programs

(13) (a) The selection of subject matter and treatment of themes should be wholesome and fresh in outlook. The more sordid aspects of life must not be emphasized.

(b) The following in particular should be avoided:

(i) torture or suggestion of torture;

(ii) horror or undue suspense;

(iii) the use of the supernatural or superstition so as to arouse anxiety or fear;

(iv) any matter likely to lead to hysteria, nightmares, or other undesirable emotional disturbances in children;

(v) excessive violence.

Children's Programs

(14) Programs televised specifically for children must comply not only with the general program standards and the standards for family programs, but also with the following special standards:

(a) All scripts must be carefully written, having in mind the needs of the particular age-groups for which the programs are intended;

(b) All stories must reflect respect for law and order, responsible adult authority, good morals, and clean living. Themes should stress fair play and honourable behaviour. Cowardice, malice, deceit, selfishness, and disrespect for the law must be avoided in the delineation of any character presented as a hero. Characterization which degrades womanhood is to be avoided, particularly in relation to the depiction of a mother;

(c) In programs in which children appear as artists, care should be taken to avoid encouraging precocity in such children, who may be tempted to 'show-off';

(d) Contests and offers, which encourage children to enter strange places and to converse with strangers for any purpose, present a definite element of danger to children and must be avoided.[3]

The above excerpts represent only a small part of a worth-while publication. Action in relation to these standards should be directed to the television station in question, to the Australian Broadcasting Control Board in each State capital (or 373 Elizabeth Street, Melbourne), and to the Minister for the Media (at present Senator D. McLelland), Parliament House, Canberra, A.C.T., 2600.

4. Television Advertising Directed to Children

The Board has determined, in accordance with Section 100(4) of the Broadcasting and Television Act, that from August 1, 1973, the following standards shall apply to advertising directed to children:

(1) Children should not be directly urged to put pressure on parents to purchase the product advertised;

(2) Advertisements should accurately represent the product, and claims concerning specific product qualities should be capable of being substantiated;
(3) Advertisements must be clearly recognizable as such and separate from the presentation of program matter;
(4) Personalities or characters from children's programs should not be used to endorse or recommend products within or adjacent to children's programs;
(5) Children in advertisements should be well-mannered, well-behaved, and show respect for parents;
(6) There should be no implication that the possession of a product makes the owners superior to their peers, nor that lack of the product may lead to ridicule and contempt. No comparison should be made with last year's models or competitive makes in such a way as to make a child possessing these feel inferior;
(7) With the objective of avoiding excessive repetition in the telecasting of advertisements directed to children, a station should exercise discretion in the placement of identical advertisements within any regularly scheduled program directed to children;
(8) If a price is mentioned, the complete price of the product should be made clear, preferably both aurally and visually, and advertisements should clearly indicate the cost of those items which constitute the original purchase and additional items that must be purchased separately;
(9) Undue emphasis should not be placed on the use of such words as "only" or "just" in stating the price of the product;
(10) In the case of a product that must be assembled, this should be made clear, and where necessary, the source of power and method of operation should be indicated;
(11) Where reference is made to competitions, the applicable rules should be made clear and the value of prizes and the chances of winning should not be exaggerated;
(12) Results shown or claimed for advertised products, such as toys or games, should be attainable by an average child without an undue degree of skill;
(13) Except in the case of specific safety messages, advertisements should not portray unsafe acts or dangerous situations, e.g. children ignoring traffic regulations or conversing with strangers;
(14) Advertising of products not intended for use by children, except for gift-giving, should not be directed to children;
(15) Frightening dramatizations or effects should not be included in advertisements directed to children.

5. Advertising

More generally, advertising is guided by the Media Council of Australia which is supported by the major agencies. Their code of ethics is as follows:

(1) Advertisements must be truthful, and shall not be misleading or liable to misinterpretation;
(2) Advertisements must be clearly distinguishable as such;

(3) Advertisements must comply with Federal and State law;
(4) Advertisements of a controversial nature shall disclose their source;
(5) Scientific, statistical, or other research data quoted in advertisements shall be neither misleading nor irrelevant;
(6) Testimonials used in advertisements must honestly reflect the sentiments of the individuals represented. Claims in testimonials are subject to the same rules as other advertising;
(7) Advertising of goods or services must be for the purpose of genuinely selling those goods or services, and not for the purpose of selling substitute goods or services;
(8) Advertisements for medicines and treatments shall be subject to the rules of the "Guide to Advertising of Proprietary Medicines and Therapeutic Appliances" in addition to the rules of this Code;
(9) The intention of an advertiser who, without making an appointment, intends to call upon or to send a representative to call upon any person applying for particulars or details of any product or service advertised must be clearly stated in the advertisement;
(10) Advertisements shall not exploit the superstitious or unduly play on fear;
(11) Advertisements shall not exploit children or contain anything which might result in their physical, mental, or moral harm;
(12) Contests shall be conducted with fairness to all entrants;
(13) If the word "guarantee" is used in an advertisement, the terms of the guarantee, or the place where the guarantee may be obtained, must be clearly stated;
(14) Mail-order advertisers shall be prepared to meet any reasonable demand created by their advertising, and shall readily refund money in full to buyers with reasonable cause for dissatisfaction with their purchase or delay in delivery. The name of a mail-order advertiser shall be prominently displayed in the advertisement, and samples of goods advertised shall be available at the advertiser's place of business for public inspection during normal business-hours;
(15) Advertisements shall not disparage identifiable products, services, or advertisers.

Complaints regarding departures from this code may be directed to the firm whose products are involved, and to the advertising agency responsible to that firm. Contact with the Media Council may also be worthwhile (100 Bathurst Street, Sydney : Phone 613738).

The Advisory Committee on Children's Television Programs for the Australian Broadcasting Control Board advises:

> "Viewers' opinions about programs are welcomed. They may lead to the showing of better programs, especially for children. It is helpful to mention programs which you think are good as well as those you think are not good for children."

Parents are advised to address their remarks to the manager of the television station concerned, or to The Australian Broadcasting Control Board, 373 Elizabeth Street, Melbourne.

Appendix 3.

[Text of a widely-distributed leaflet which was prepared to assist those who are concerned about acting as responsible citizens.]

YOU AND THE PERMISSIVE SOCIETY

Sexual permissiveness is becoming almost fashionable nowadays. It is spreading like cancer through most sections of the society. Our daily press, radio, and TV seem to be encouraging this unhealthy trend.

Naturally, it is a cause of concern for parents of young children. Parents believe that this easy-going trend towards sexual morality could weaken the moral stability of their own children, and also realize that, apart from the home, current community-standards exert the greatest influence on development of attitudes and ideals of the young.

Some parents are so concerned that they ask themselves, "What can I do?", "What should I do to introduce better standards, not only in my home, but also to the community in which I live?", "Where does one start?"

Start with self

Why not start with yourself? After all, you can hardly be expected to influence others to take on better standards if **you** don't live by them. That is going to depend on you having worth-while motives.

Natural Motives

Some people may be moved only by purely natural motives. They may be swayed by such factors as human respect, orderly living, or the preservation of good health. Then you find that standards based on natural motives will vary from person to person, depending on their own point of view. For example, "free love" can be considered acceptable if there is mutual agreement and neither partner is exploited.

Religious Motives

Other people are moved to introduce better standards into daily life by religious motives based on fixed moral principles. Religiously-moved people see others in a new dimension — to be protected rather than exploited. They see the human body as "God's temple", and this gives the human form a sacredness. They see every bodily power as having its own noble purpose.

Once a person begins thinking along these lines, he gets some idea of the dignity of the human person. Therefore, standards of human behaviour should be in keeping with it. Unfortunately, the world has lost the ability to see this dignity in the human person.

As far as the world is concerned, it is simply human convenience that decides standards of human behaviour, and it is in this sort of world that the individual today can take a stand for decency and help introduce higher values into a world that has lost them.

Better Community Standards Can Be Fostered By You

AS A PARENT — by providing excellence of example. Bringing only quality reading matter into the home. Ensuring a sound sex instruction based on respect for the opposite sex. Pornography and indecency thrive on ignorance.

Encouraging interest in music and the arts. Filling young minds with the better things in life will give less opportunity for sordid things to take hold.

By encouraging any child with creative writing talent to take up a career of writing. The power of the media to uplift and inspire humanity is tremendous. A virtual handful of thousands of writers are creating material for the TV, the press, literature, and films, so the thinking of millions is controlled by a few. Therefore, a crying need exists for writers of integrity.

AS A WORKER — steering conversation away from indecent talk. Removing magazines and calendars that might be a cause of embarrassment to women or a source of provocation to young men.

AS A MEMBER OF A POLITICAL PARTY — drawing attention to the need for more effective obscenity laws and for constant vigilance on the part of the law-enforcement authorities — police, Customs Department, etc.

AS A CONSUMER — making views known to business firms regarding advertising campaigns. Be positive, and praise worthy aspects of an ad., when registering disapproval.

Support commodities advertised in a dignified way.

AS A CUSTOMER OF A NEWSAGENCY — congratulating the proprietor if sex-laden magazines and paper-backs are not given prominence. Summon courage and make your views known if his display is offensive.

Organized deputations of combined church and civic groups have been effective in encouraging retailers to exercise discrimination in what they accept from publishers and distributors.

AS A FILM GOER — Support of quality films is registering a vote of approval to managers, distributors, and producers. Familiarize yourself with newspaper critiques to be in a position to recommend better films to your teenagers.

Stress to these young people the uplifting and exhilarating effect of a film like "Sound of Music", as against the depressing and wretched feelings that result from erotic films.

Register your views on films that over-emphasize sex and violence to The Commonwealth Film Censor, Castlereagh Street, Sydney, 2000.

AS A READER — You can render a valuable service if you do all in your power to help make newspapers and magazines more effective communications of truth and wholesomeness.

A well-deserved "pat on the back" for the reporters, columnists, authors, and editors who provide quality reading is a most effective way of ensuring better standards. Letters to the editor can have far-reaching effect. People read these, and, naturally, are influenced by them. A potential audience of hundreds of thousands is readily available. *Even unpublished letters can influence future editorial policy.*

Make your views about film advertisements known to the general manager of the paper.

AS AN INDIVIDUAL — Realize and point out that each person can strengthen or weaken public morality. Remind others that every dollar spent on literature and entertainment is a vote for or against decency and true artistic achievement. We are made for society, and it is society which makes us. By your manner of dress, talk, and your general behaviour, you can make society just a little better; and society being just a little improved, in turn helps to make the individual a little better. Unfortunately, this process can work in reverse, to the detriment of society and the individual.

AS A CITIZEN — Congratulate police and government officials controlling literature, films, TV, when action is taken for better community-standards. Encourage them to take further steps to protect our impressionable and vulnerable youth.

AS A TV WATCHER — Select only quality programs. This will influence children more than lectures. Be aware of your responsibility to know what is available to your youngster and what they are viewing.

Report questionable matter on commercial TV or national TV. A single call or letter is recognized as equivalent to hundreds who would have similar views but do not bother to act. (Address in telephone book.)

AS A BUSINESS OR PROFESSIONAL MAN — Enrich your company's image by using tasteful advertising. Decency gains respect from the community at large and is good business.

Codes of ethics can be drafted, revised, or enforced to outlaw suggestive material.

Be sure that reading matter in waiting-rooms is of a high calibre.

AS A TEACHER OR YOUTH WORKER — Good schools, good libraries, good music, good sport — these help to influence tastes and values towards higher rather than lower levels.

> "Educational efforts towards overcoming mental slothfulness and satisfaction with mediocrity, toward developing the varied talents of a person for vocational usefulness to himself and others, and toward minimizing the normal tendencies to selfish satisfactions, are constructive steps of a long-range nature." (U.S. Senate Sub-Committee on Obscene Literature.)

AS A SHAREHOLDER — In any company which features doubtful material, you, as a shareholder, have definite rights and your comments will be listened to.

AS A HUMANITARIAN — Give more thought to the lonely, demoralized people of the community — the delinquents, divorcees, abandoned wives, unmarried mothers, independent youth living away from the restraining influence of the home, the drop-outs of society who couldn't keep up the pace.

Often the frustrations of these people drive them to accept fallen standards.

TAKE COURAGE, HAVE AN OPINION, AND
MAKE YOUR VOICE HEARD

Appendix 4

[It is easy to observe changes. It is also easy to criticize declining standards. The challenge then comes in identifying what standards are wanted.

The following statement was prepared by a large group of well-informed citizens from many walks of life, all supporting the aims of the Festival of Light. Men and women, young and old, from a wide range of church affiliations, political parties, and social backgrounds, contributed to the wording of this statement. It is reproduced here with the conviction that it deserves wider circulation than it received when first presented on October 14, 1973. In that all contributors expressed a Christian conviction, the statement may be read as an attempt to represent that unchanging standard which comes from Biblical revelation.]

This Festival is one of a number of festivals around the world expressing the concern of many people at declining standards of morality, with consequent harm to individuals and to the community. The term "Festival" has been chosen to emphasise that we are more interested in proclamation than protest, in making positive recommendations than in criticism. Nevertheless if light is to shine, darkness must be exposed. We are therefore identifying areas of life where undesirable influences are at work, and pointing towards solutions. We do not see this as a final statement, but one designed to alert people to problems. It is a preliminary statement about what might be done, preparing the way for further effort in a continuing Festival which will draw together men and women who see the need for concerted action.

We recognize that all who will stand for what is true and good run the risk of abuse and ridicule from those whose defence of evil is thereby challenged. We therefore urge those who care, to stand firm with humility, avoiding arrogance and ill-informed dogmatism, but remaining firm where clear moral principles must be maintained. Courtesy to, and respect for, those with whom one may disagree are themselves indicators of the recognition of the rights of others which deserve to be respected.

We take our stand in the strong conviction that we represent the aspirations of the overwhelming majority of decent people, who have, for too long, been confused by the empty promises of a vocal minority.

The greatest support is undoubtedly from those of Christian conviction who see a real threat to Christian standards of morality which have been the basis for our national way of life. For Christians this Festival is an opportunity to proclaim Jesus Christ as the Light of the world. So, too, in identifying the problems of "moral pollution", Christians proclaim that not only do they need a solution but that there is one to be found in following Christ.

Non-Christians have also expressed support for the Festival for various reasons, and seeing the same social evils, are looking for answers.

In proclaiming the importance of moral standards, we stress that we are not simply concerned about sexual attitudes or behaviour. In expressing our concern for human and family life, we believe that high moral standards are essential in such areas as commerce, mass media, education, industrial relationships, and racial attitudes. Troubles in all these areas suggest that the moral problems of our society have deep roots. The Christian assessment of man as made by God, and of his individual value before God, therefore underlies much of what follows.

The following statements have not been subjected to unanimous agreement by all identifying themselves with the Festival, but arise from the recommendations of a large and well-qualified committee. In part, we have also drawn with appreciation on statements prepared by the nation-wide Festival of Light in Britain.

We now present them as the basis for further action by those supporting the Festival, as well as for the attention of those groups to whom we specifically address ourselves. This is a time of social change, and because not all change is equally beneficial, we believe that this is the right time to draw attention to the needs of individuals and families in Australia.

Initially the Festival of Light set itself four tasks:

(i) To unite the Churches and all concerned people in a positive act of witness in the community;

(ii) To alert Australians and inform them of the dangers of moral pollution;

(iii) To translate into action the concern that many have about the lowering of moral standards in home and national life today;

(iv) To make national leaders aware that a large proportion of the population is anxious to preserve Christian moral standards.

It has continued in the conviction that many people, troubled about the moral climate of society, wish to affirm their belief in and desire for a wholesome society as a happy society.

The focus of this Festival is on the family. Among the many structures which deserve careful attention in contemporary society, we have selected the family as an essential unit currently threatened by many forces. We believe survival of the family is essential both for the welfare of the young and for the cohesion of society. It is imperative that we prevent the family either from disintegrating inadvertently, or from being deliberately overthrown. Our statements will therefore be presented with special reference to the need to strengthen and maintain sound family structures.

The Festival of Light affirms that the well-being of society depends on the moral goodness of people and their sense of responsibility. It affirms that the qualities basic to any wholesome and happy society are honesty, fidelity, purity, gentleness, care for others, and responsibility. It aims to give support to all people of goodwill, especially in the fields of education, entertainment, the media, and politics who wish to see virtue, not vice, glorified, and goodness, not badness, encouraged. The Festival of Light says to everyone, "Let us all lift the quality of our moral contribution to society and see the difference it makes".

To fulfil these aims, we are therefore addressing ourselves to four groups — those in (i) the Churches, (ii) the community at large, (iii) media, and (iv) our Governments.

1. TO THE CHURCHES

We speak first with a note of critical self-examination. While recognizing the powerfully-good influence of Christian teaching in Australia, we acknowledge that many of the challenges to full commitment and sacrificial involvement have not been faced.

As a result, our nation is spiritually weak and in moral danger. We have spoken of the need to follow Christ, but in practice have followed him comfortably rather than sacrificially. By saying but not doing, we find men look upon us as blind guides with no light to shine.

We have been cautious in calling men to repentance, fearing it is old-fashioned and judgemental. We are slow to repent ourselves, except in small matters. We have grown comfortable in our affluent society, and so find it hard to challenge those values and attitudes which treat possessions and power as more important than people.

We, therefore, reaffirm that we have a responsibility to be involved in the affairs of the world in which we live. Now is the moment for all Christians to respond constructively to lowered moral values. We see the need to be both salt and light in society. It is our vocation not only to shed abroad the light of God's love, but also to exercise the beneficial influence of salt in a corrupt society.

"There is no end to loving others. We may not be 'personally' responsible for the world's poverty and misery, but we are collectively responsible. And collective responsibility necessitates a collective effort to fulfil that responsiblity." (Quoist)

Ultimately, this responsibility must be met in terms of each individual who has unique value in the eyes of God. Anything which would undermine human dignity or prevent a person from facing his personal responsibilities before God is a proper cause for Christian concern.

We urge all Christians to be faithful in proclaiming God's laws for all men, so that a clear lead is given in distinguishing good from evil.

We cannot remain involved only with our own affairs, as we have been clearly instructed to go into all the world and preach the Gospel. We must bring the Gospel to men and women in terms of their present needs. We must challenge those who would disregard God and refuse to accept His salvation as the only sufficient solution.

Recognizing the importance of preparation for marriage and family life, we urge greater support for those groups in the community already committed to this task. We also urge Churches, individually and collectively, to make more adequate provision for marriage preparation and counselling through which Christian principles of family living may be communicated. We cannot complain at secular sex-education programs, devoid of moral values, if we fail to take the initiative in offering preparation for living.

II: TO THE COMMUNITY

No one lives to himself. It is naive and false to assume that the behaviour and attitudes of individuals affect none but themselves. The actions of each person influence others and filter through to society as a whole. Every one who makes a stand for truth and goodness makes a worthwhile contribution to the common good.

We firmly believe that individuals are entitled to their rights. We give wholehearted support to personal freedom provided it is balanced by a sense of responsibility and takes account of the importance of human relationships. Our responsibility extends to understanding others and the nature of the society in which we live. It includes being true to what we believe, even when this is costly. Our relationships, to be constructive, must be caring ones; and at all levels — family, social, industrial — we must stand against exploitation of others.

We play our proper part in society as we recognize that all have a contribution to make. Too often, we assume that, because ours is a lone voice, any comment or witness or protest we make will be futile. We must acknowledge that the silence of others may spring from our own reticence. This Festival is a demonstration that the active concern of a few can mobilize the hidden wishes of many.

It is not sufficient to be critical of what we see around us. A constructive approach will be both negative and positive. We cannot escape the need for specific protest, informed criticism, and recourse to law. Such counter-action must be balanced by morally sound initiatives in demonstrating the value of what is good and true and honest. This demands integrity of action as well as words, if the trap of double-standards is to be avoided.

At the present time the prevalence of morally-corrupt influences presents a special challenge. The greater the darkness, the greater the opportunity for light to shine. "All that is needed for evil to triumph is that good men do nothing." (Burke)

(a) Family and Work

We therefore seek to alert the community to significant inroads into traditional standards of morality. In particular:

(i) We reaffirm that the family is the basic unit of society, and call attention to the need both to strengthen it and to resist those influences which are undermining it;

(ii) We believe in the special care of children so that they shall be protected from exploitation and unwarranted intrusion into their privacy;

(iii) We assert that much present-day advertising is degrading to the dignity of women, and call for more responsible control over this explicit commercialization of sex;

(iv) No man or woman should be subjected to work-relationships which degrade their existence to mere instruments of production, whatever the pattern of economic organization. While repetitive tasks may continue to be necessary, their effects on individuals are often damaging to family-life. Workers need opportunities to be involved in the design and control of productive processes, while the associated needs of families should be taken into account,

(v) Equality of opportunity should be expressed in any economic system, with needs and rewards being taken into account in the distribution of wealth. The needs of people and families, with attention to quality of life and provision of community care, deserve priority;

(vi) In welcoming the increased opportunities for leisure arising from technological development, we see a need to assist families and groups in ensuring that leisure activities develop so that they focus positively on human needs and aspirations;

(vii) Believing in the fundamental principle of equality of worth of all human beings, we deplore discrimination based on race, wealth, sex, or cultural groups. Discrimination limits human dignity, and frustrates the building of an open, caring, forgiving community.

(b) To Parents

Healthy life and growth are dependent upon influences in the lives of children as they grow, and their response to them. These influences must permit full expression of uniqueness and the growing realization of their potential. At the same time they must be provided with sufficient security and consistent guidelines so that growth is purposeful.

Essential to this process are other people. Actions and reactions to others lie at the heart of the ability of children to find fulfilment. Healthy growth is only possible when the behaviour of the individual is modified by the influence of other people, whose rights and drives for fulfilment one must come to respect. These are first met in the family circle, then in teachers, leaders, communicators, etc., and finally, in the world-community at large. The growing child will normally find himself only in relationships with others. Independence must mature into inter-dependence.

In this process the stable home and family is indispensable. The stability and warmth of a good marriage at the centre, then healthy relationships between parents and children, with inter-relationships where there is neither carelessness or oppression, are the ideals towards which we must strive — and influence the community to make these goals more attainable.

(c) Family and Education

We seek a style of education which will turn the thinking of the nation away from callousness, apathy, and immaturity. These are all consequences of living simply for self-gratification and the desire to exploit others, which is the essence of pornography.

It is the aim of education to create a community which faces the world's needs, with the attributes of sensitivity, responsibility, skill in creating the conditions of world peace, and skill in creating a world society that works to end hunger, disease, poverty, and callousness.

Education is more efficient and better financed than ever before. Yet in many ways we are worse-off than we were thirty years ago. In terms of suicide, divorce, delinquency, and psychiatric disorders, the extent of human unhappiness is very great.

Psychiatrists are unanimous about the vital importance of the first few years of life in determining the social and mental future of the child — for better or for worse.

Most education does not occur in school at all. Modern children spend at least as much time in front of the TV as they do in the classroom. We ought therefore to be at least as careful to ensure high standards of home viewing as to ensure good educational facilities for our children.

Preschool centres cannot provide a completely satisfactory alternative to a stable home. Staff turnover, even in the best institutions, precludes the permanence that is so important in a child's relationships with his parents.

Nor are remedial programs the solution, since damage in early childhood is very hard to correct later.

The callow philosophy of the so-called "permissive approach" ignores the needs of others. The mask of a philosophy of self-gratification is soft and inviting, but its reality is hard and cruel — as hard and cruel as selfishness.

We must direct more educational resources to parents and future parents, (e.g. courses on marriage and parenthood) since so many of the critical experiences in a child's life occur in the home.

We must teach children positive attitudes towards marriage and family-life. Mere instruction in sexual techniques is sadly inadequate, and, without parallel education in human relationships, will do more harm than good. Instruction must be appropriate to their level of development and understanding, and the danger of intruding on the natural defences of reticence and modesty must be carefully avoided.

Educational practice must be assessed to ensure that these principles are re-inforced in every area. Books which openly or subtly advocate irresponsibility and transience in sexual relationships (and hence marriage and families) should have no place in our curriculums.

As teachers are increasingly free to experiment with new ideas in education, they bear a greater responsibility to be alert to the emotional needs of the children they teach.

This freedom can bring great enrichment to children, but it must also be exercised carefully.

There can be no justification for deliberately shocking, embarrassing, or intruding on the private sensitivities of students.

III. TO THE MASS MEDIA

(a) Television

We recognize television to be among the most powerful psychological influences in contemporary society. Therefore the responsibility rests on licensee and viewer alike to use it constructively. The presentation of programs inevitably involves some degree of selection which, unless completely random, must operate according to certain principles.

We give support to the existing guidelines of the Australian Broadcasting Control Board relating to programming and advertising, but seek that these guidelines be applied more rigorously in recognition that television has such a significant place in the family setting.

We note that the standards prescribed apply only to commercial stations and believe that the same principles should be required of the ABC.

While welcoming as a significant advance the recent guidelines relating to advertising to children on television, we note that Australia is one of the very few countries in the world that allows any advertising in children's viewing-time. Children are vulnerable, easily exploited, and deserve protection from unwarranted commercial pressures: such advertising is unwarranted.

Recognizing the great potential of TV as a "window on the world", showing events around us in dramatic fashion, we regret the imbalance which so frequently occurs. Seeing the needs of others could move us to help, but too often the camera lingers on the sensational, the violent, and the bizarre. The normal and healthy receive disproportionately little attention. Stable family life appears most infrequently.

Much more should be made of the educational potential of TV in exploring and explaining the world, e.g. in helping people to come to grips with social problems and problems of relationships.

There needs to be far more research and development of the educational potential of TV for children. It can have many positive benefits, as some American TV educational (and entertaining) children's programs have shown. Many educational TV programs used in schools warrant inclusion in the family-viewing time-slot. We would like to see more programs which give children a sense of personal worth and pride in individuality, presenting good models for emulation.

Current affairs programs can educate the viewer and help him to evaluate several sides of questions. There need to be more programs where many issues are freely explored by reasonably-impartial interviewers.

In the entertainment field, TV could show us the best of what the world has to offer in music, drama, humour, etc., and to appreciate the creativity of others. But the scene is dominated by the "formula" drama, the trivial variety show, and by the interminable quizzes which feed on and foster greed. Panels of pretty people pronouncing on other people's problems could better be replaced by panels who really care about counselling or who have some wisdom to offer to the many troubled people who watch.

There is a need for more stimulating programs for women in daytime viewing. Current affairs and news programs from the previous night's early-evening viewing could be replayed the following day for the benefit of mothers who feel that they should spend the early-evening hours with their children.

The standard of our drama programs needs raising and the topics need expanding. There is a need for good drama which conveys some aspect of truth about life, and gives people insight into the feelings and problems, joys and delights of others. Most of current drama overemphasizes a few areas of life such as sex and violence, and censors by omission vast areas of human experience — e.g. happy marriages, marital fidelity, Christian life and work. The effect of many current programs is to undermine faith and moral standards.

A striking example of moral pollution in our time is the excessive presentation of violence on the screen. Both films and television present violence with a realism that is compelling, whether based on fact or fiction. Increasing evidence shows clearly that many children and disturbed adults respond to this by increasing their own aggressive behaviour. Others lose an appropriate response to violence.

We stress that TV is, for the majority of viewers, a learning situation in a domestic setting. Young children can be deeply distressed by television violence. Most children today largely fashion their own picture of the wider world of adult life in terms of what they see on television. They can be seriously misled about the amount of violence in society. Older children vicariously enjoy the thrills of a violent life-style such that TV tends to legitimize violence. Improvements in the quality of television must take seriously the need to bring the portrayal of violence into perspective. Such a need is even more pressing than the desire to increase Australian content.

We also wish to give wide publicity to the Australian Broadcasting Control Board's recommendations on standards including "the overriding obligation of licensees to avoid televising program material which can give offence to sections of the public or can be harmful to the young people who make up a large part of the audience at certain times of day".

High standards need to be maintained not only during children's or family viewing-time. "The basic requirements which must always be observed in the presentation of television programs are that: no program may contain any matter which is contrary to law, blasphemous, indecent, or obscene; likely to encourage crime; likely to be injurious to community well-being or morality; or otherwise undesirable in the public interest."

(b) Films

The trend to violence among films is also a matter for concern. A restricted classification does not provide adequate protection for the community against those disturbed adults who seek out the violence of contemporary films, only to act out their fantasies later. The clear imitation of violence, especially of the "A Clockwork Orange" type, is the visible evidence of much more which threatens the freedom of ordinary citizens to walk the streets.

Violence in all the media is not only physical; it can be verbal. We are disturbed to find increasing use of words in books, films, and on TV, which come from the most violent register of English obscene abuse. That such words (commonly called four-letter Anglo-Saxon) are known to the vast majority of males in the community in no way justifies a wide acceptance or usage.

These words are not equivalents for conventional terms. Their use is frequently a form of verbal assault. Their widespread acceptance can too easily result in an overall debasement of experience as children come to incorporate them into their vocabulary. In addition, adults under stress may find themselves deprived of their final, most powerful non-physical resources and, hence, be driven to physical violence instead.

We seek a restoration of freedom to choose entertainment from a range of films which is not saturated with sexual obsession.

We express our deep concern at the proposals to extend the range of films available in this country to include pornographic material in an "unclassified" category. While such a policy is consistent with a wish to allow complete personal freedom, it conflicts with the need for responsibility in restraining some persons for the good of all.

(c) Radio

We express our support for the way in which radio is being widely used for information and education. In particular, we appreciate the good quality of responsible talk-back which is characteristic of radio in South Australia. Such programs are of special value to the aged and lonely, the housewife, and those with personal problems to discuss.

We note that in other places radio has suffered from sex-orientated talk-backs of an undesirable type. We urge vigilance against the introduction of such into this State.

We draw attention to the increasing number of records beamed to the teenage market which emphasize and endorse drug-taking; we urge parents and their children to combat this trend together.

(d) Books and magazines

The growth of pornography in the media is one of the most conspicuously destructive influences in our community. Books, magazines, and films have all been allowed circulation in recent years which previously were restrained. The defence of prevailing community standards is a dubious one at a time when commercial interests are so well able to shape public opinion to accept uncritically what would otherwise have been rejected.

Offence to the ordinary citizen has now become widespread. While modesty and reticence have discouraged many people from making public protest, this Festival aims to give open expression to the need to respect the sensitivities of others. We ask for freedom to shop without encountering offensive books. We deplore the trend in popular magazines towards the trivialization of human experience, and assert that there remains a good market for literature of quality.

We do not seek repressive censorship of any kind of material, because we recognize the dangers inherent in this. However, when pollution of the mind becomes so widespread through the various media, quality control becomes as important as for our food and drink. The good must be promoted, so the bad will die.

Restraint on the proliferation of pornography and the destructive influence of promiscuity must be exercised for the sake of the family. Promotion of "swinging" (i.e. promiscuity) is an example of the obsession with non-relational sex which reacts to the detriment both of those who engage in it, and those around who condone it. Marital fidelity is a cardinal principle of Christian teaching.

(e) Newspapers

We call on the press to accept the responsibility of presenting balanced news reports, and to avoid slanting articles for political or entertainment purposes. We ask that they continue to expose evil practices without using these as an excuse to over-emphasize damaging material.

We urge newspapers to follow the example of radio talk-backs in giving more space to contributors, thus reflecting the views of all sections of the community.

We strongly object to the exploitation of women by presenting them as objects to advertise goods, and to the commercial exploitation of human perversion and weakness.

We urge greater restraint by daily papers in the publication of advertisements on entertainment pages which currently cause offence in many homes.

All the media have a responsibility to present the news fairly, with an important part to play in helping people to understand issues which affect them. We believe they must always remain independent of government control in order to call attention to e.g. injustice, corruption, and bureaucratic neglect. We urge that such freedom shall not be abused by presenting with approval that which would promote crime or denigrate human relationships. In the long run, people matter more than scoops.

IV. TO THE GOVERNMENT

In relation to the family unit we draw attention to the Universal Declaration of Human Rights (Article 16 (3)):

> "The family is the natural and fundamental group-unit of society and is entitled to protection by society and the State."

We therefore seek assurance that legislation which affects the family-unit be framed with due recognition of this principle. Clearly, matters like divorce reform, age of marriage, provision for single mothers, and child-care facilities, all come within this area.

Other legislation dealing with the employment of women, taxation arrangements, housing policies, and provision for the aged, will influence the quality of family life. Strengthening of families (not simply the nuclear-family) deserves priority above other economic or political pressures.

In a society where adults are often selfish and pre-occupied, much has been said of children's rights. We believe the upbringing of children must remain the responsibility of parents. They need assistance from the law if this responsibility is to be exercised conscientiously. We emphasize the special needs of children which should influence legislation.

In particular, we refer to the UNICEF Declaration of the Rights of the Child, whose Principle 2 states:

> "the child shall enjoy special protection, and shall be given opportunities and facilities, by law and by other means, to enable him to develop physically, mentally, morally, spiritually, and socially in a healthy and normal manner and in conditions of freedom and dignity. In the enactment of laws for this purpose the best interests of the child shall be the paramount consideration".

We believe that the concept of "victimless crimes" is potentially hazardous to family life. The phrase is a contradiction in terms. To abolish legal constraints on prostitution, bigamy, and incest, could only have a destructive impact on family life.

V. CONCLUSION

We stand for the dignity of each person as a creature of God. We believe each human being is entitled to be treated as an individual in his own right and to develop whatever talents and abilities he possesses to their fullest extent, subject to his existence as a social being.

Man's opportunity for personal development has never been greater, but pressures brought to bear by various elements in our social environment discourage this development. He is encouraged by pornography and violence in entertainment and literature to seek self-gratification rather than self-development. Our society is developing a culture based largely on permissive sex and violence.

The explicit sex depicted in many of our films and literature degrades man's dignity by undermining the significance of the personal relationship and by disregarding mutual respect.

We believe that the society which offers most to its members is a society which upholds the values of a strong, healthy, happy family life — a society which upholds the sacred relationship of husband and wife, and of parents and their children.

We abhor the obvious attacks being perpetrated against these ideals — attacks aimed at the very nature of the family, the sacredness of sexual love in marriage, and the freedom of parents to instil in their children true Christian values.

> "When bad men combine, the good must associate; else they will fall, one by one, an unpitied sacrifice in a contemptible struggle." (Burke)

In contrast to the present vogue for slavish self-centredness, we believe the ideal of unselfish service for others needs re-emphasis.

We are expecting our education system to do many things which should be done in the home and merely modified at school. We expect our children to be honest and hardworking when the example given to them condones cheating and stealing from the community. As a society we are accepting this behaviour as normal. We are passing off our responsibilities to others and condoning those things that are harmful because it is convenient to do so. We remain apathetic to our peril.

We therefore call upon the people of South Australia, individually and collectively, to accept the responsibilities of citizenship and care for others by becoming involved, active, and vocal.

Index